HOW TO MANAGE
WITH CLARITY AN

The Mindful Budget

GRACE ALLISON

Copyright © 2020 Grace Allison.

All rights reserved. No part of this book may be reproduced, stored, or transmitted by any means—whether auditory, graphic, mechanical, or electronic—without written permission of both publisher and author, except in the case of brief excerpts used in critical articles and reviews. Unauthorized reproduction of any part of this work is illegal and is punishable by law.

ISBN: 979-8-6992-70255

Cover design by 100Covers
Interior design by FormattedBooks

Contents

Introduction v

Step One: Know your Money 1

Step Two: Plan Your Money 25

Step Three: Spend your Money 55

Step Four: Save Your Money 79

Step Five: Enjoy Your Money 89

Appendix 1 93

Introduction

Have you ever had the disconcerting experience of getting to the end of the day and realising that you have no idea where the hours went? Perhaps there is a little less cookie-dough ice cream in the freezer, leaving you with some kind of clue about how the day was spent, but nothing more. 'Where on earth did all of that time *go?*' you ask yourself.

Similarly, all of us at some point in our lives will find ourselves wondering, 'Where on earth did all of that *money* go?'

The reason for both of these phenomena is not that we have some kind of cookie-dough-ice-cream-induced amnesia or are irresponsible spenders. The reason is that both time and money are resources that can easily slip through our fingers when we don't have a plan for them.

If you want to make the most of your day, you need some way to structure your time: a routine. If you want to make the most of your money … you need a budget.

You need a budget, but you don't need my budget

If you were trying to follow someone else's daily routine, it would be a pretty pointless, frustrating endeavour. Why would you spend an hour every day carefully pruning a bonsai collection when your passion is making jewellery?

The same is true for a budget. I can't tell you what your budget should look like. I don't know how much value you get out of your ribbon collection, and therefore how much you should spend on it. I don't know whether you have a dog, a cat or three small children. Your budget is as personal to you as your daily routine.

What you *do* need is a budgeting method. You need a framework for gathering all of your financial information in one place, creating a plan that will work for you and, most importantly, *sticking to that plan.*

THE MINDFUL BUDGET METHOD

Before I describe the five steps of the Mindful Budget method, here are some definitions that will be useful for understanding my approach.

Budget
A budget is the end result, the *product* of the process of budgeting. A budget can be an Excel spreadsheet, a beautiful, hand-illustrated page in your journal, a thick folder with colour-coded dividers for every month, or simply a scribble on the back of an envelope. Of course, it is perfectly possible for a budget to exist entirely in your head. However, for the purposes of learning, I believe it is important to create a physical budget of some kind to show your process and to use as a reference.

Budgeting
Budgeting is a skill. It is the ability to take all of your financial information and turn it into a plan for your money. But budgeting is not just about making a plan, it is also about sticking to that plan and adapting and refining it over time to achieve your financial goals. The purpose of this book is to guide you into becoming a more skilled budgeter.

Mindfulness
Mindfulness is the practice of awareness: awareness of the present moment and everything that you are currently experiencing. You can incorporate mindfulness into any aspect of your life. If you are interested, I would highly recommend learning more about this grounding and deeply helpful practice.

Mindful Budgeting

Mindful budgeting is the practice of budgeting in an honest, reflective and non-judgmental manner. It is about accepting the financial situation that you find yourself in right now. It is about knowing what truly brings you value. When you make mistakes, there is no need to beat yourself up about them. Simply acknowledge that they happened and move on.

THE FIVE STEPS

The Mindful Budget method consists of five simple steps. Each chapter of this book will walk you through one of the five steps.

Step One: Know Your Money
Know how much money you have and what you want to do with it.

Step Two: Plan Your Money
How to make a plan for every pound, dollar or euro that you earn.

Step Three: Spend Your Money
Discover three tools that will ensure you actually stick to your budget.

Step Four: Save Your Money
Three simple ways to make saving a habit that you can enjoy.

Step Five: Enjoy Your Money
How to find financial peace by letting go of the stress and worry surrounding money.

HOW TO GET THE MOST OUT OF THIS BOOK

In the following chapters I will lead you through a specific budgeting method. To illustrate my points, I will be using images of the same spreads and trackers that I use in my planner for my own personal finances. All of the spreads you see in this book are available to download for free by following this link to

The Mindful Budget Bundle[1], or you can simply follow along using a blank piece of paper.

Of course, I'm not arrogant enough to think that this is the only method for managing your finances. However, it is the simplest, most comprehensive framework that I have found to teach all of the necessary skills for becoming a proficient budgeter. My advice is to stick as closely as you can to the method laid out in this book as you create your first few budgets. You will not only gain better control over your money in the short term but, by applying the method to your own finances, you will begin to understand the process. As you get more and more proficient, you will be able to adapt and refine this method so that your budget is perfectly tailored to suit you.

Paper Versus Digital

Should you create your budget with pen and paper or in a digital spreadsheet? There is no definitive answer because both methods have their benefits and drawbacks. However, the Mindful Budget method favours pen and paper. This is especially true when it comes to getting started on your budgeting journey.

One of the most common reasons that people struggle to keep on top of their finances is because money can seem very abstract. This is especially true when it is in a digital or electronic format. It is easy for debit cards and online shopping to run away from us because we never actually see the money leave our wallets.

The Mindful Budget makes use of old-fashioned pen and paper, as well as physical cash in physical envelopes, to help you get back on track with your spending. Give it a go – you might be surprised at the results.

MEET THE CAST

It can be difficult (not to mention extremely dull) to understand detailed, specific advice about budgeting without seeing it carried out in practice. To help illustrate the concepts that I will be explaining, I make use throughout the book of examples taken from three case studies.

---

[1] https://downloads.grace-allison.com/mindful-budget-bundle

Tess

Tess is twenty-five years old. She is a dental nurse and lives in a shared house in Bristol with two other friends. Although Tess really enjoys her job, her big dream is to cycle from Bangkok to London with her housemate, Clara. Tess is very proud of her Japanese heritage and spends a lot of time (and money) making delicious, authentic Japanese food. She recently discovered CrossFit and goes to the 'box' four days a week.

Cami

Cami is twenty-two years old. She graduated with an engineering degree three months ago. She hasn't found her first job in engineering yet, so she has taken on two part-time jobs: one in a pub, and one in a children's shoe shop. Even though she makes an effort to live frugally, Cami is shocked at the way her money seems to disappear every month. She wants to get on top of her spending and build good financial habits before she moves into her profession. Cami lives in a shared flat in Sheffield and has a boyfriend, Mark, who lives nearby. Cami and Mark do their finances separately but they share a passion for rock climbing and a black lab called Otter.

Adam and Ayesha

Adam is twenty-eight years old and Ayesha is twenty-seven. Adam is a history teacher and Ayesha is a self-employed graphic designer. They live together in a rented house in the north of England. Their dream is to own their own home (outright, with no mortgage) and to start a family. They are ready to throw everything they have into making this dream a reality.

As you read this book, you will get an in-depth look at the finances of these four people. The figures that I've used were accurate at the time this book was written, but don't get too caught up in the actual amounts (or the currency, if you are from another part of the world!). What is more important is the way their stories demonstrate the *process* of creating a budget that is tailored to an individual's circumstances and goals.

Step One
KNOW YOUR MONEY

The number one reason that budgets fail is because they miss out important information. It's all very well creating a budget filled only with what you would ideally like to spend on food, transport and going out, etc. But if those figures don't align with your true needs, then it's not going to work. It won't be sustainable. And if you forget to include necessary expenses, like council tax or your water bill, you won't have a true picture of what you can afford. You won't actually know if you are on track to achieve your financial goals.

There is no shame in a budget that fails. We all make mistakes. You just try again next month. What *is* a shame, however, is when you feel like a failure because your budget didn't meet your needs. If you feel bad about your experience, you might give up and miss out on all of the benefits that budgeting has to offer.

The best way to avoid this feeling of failure is to start your budget by getting all of your information in one place. Using that information, you can make a plan that works and stick to it. Success!

In this section you will answer the following questions:

- Why are you making a budget?
- Where is all of your money right now?
- How much do you make and when do you get paid?

- What are your current spending habits?
- What fixed expenses are due and when?
- What big expenses do you need to set aside money for?
- What do you owe in debt?
- What are your savings goals?

Answering these questions will give you all of the information to create your first budget. You can use the spread included in the free Mindful Budget Bundle[2] download, or you can write your answers on paper.

Remember, the focus of this budget method is *mindfulness*. This means being honest, reflective and non-judgmental. Until you acknowledge and accept your current financial situation, you can't make changes and improvements in the future.

WHY ARE YOU MAKING A BUDGET?

Who is the person in your life, that you are willing to make real sacrifices for? What is that one thing that you always find yourself daydreaming about on the bus, or as you drift off to sleep?

For Tess, that thing is a once-in-a-lifetime adventure, cycling all the way across Asia and Europe. For Cami, those things are climbing with her boyfriend and her dog, Otter. Cami and Mark want to save up for their own, self-built camper van which will open up a whole new world of climbing trips for them. For Adam and Ayesha, that thing is building their life together. They want to own their home and start a family.

WHERE IS ALL OF YOUR MONEY RIGHT NOW?

First, make a list of all of your bank accounts, including savings accounts, ISAs, building society accounts, pensions and credit cards. If you keep a balance with services like PayPal and Apple Pay, write those down too. Make sure to include any joint accounts that you are part of.

---

[2] https://downloads.grace-allison.com/mindful-budget-bundle

Next, write down the balances of all these accounts. Obviously, money in any joint accounts does not belong solely to you, but it is part of your financial situation so write it down.

Finally, find all of your spare change and dig up any gift cards, vouchers or pre-paid cards that you have lying around. Write these amounts down, too.

Once everything is written down in one place, it makes it easier to visualise your situation and to make a plan.

HOW MUCH DO YOU MAKE AND WHEN DO YOU GET PAID?

If you have a full-time job that pays you once a month, then this part is very straightforward. Simply add your take-home salary (the amount that lands in your account after tax and National Insurance) and the date that you get paid.

If you have multiple sources of income or get paid on a different schedule (for example, weekly), it is even more important to be on top of your incomings and outgoings. Write down every income source, the amount that it pays and when it arrives.

Sometimes you might not always know the exact amount to expect from a particular source. In that case, use an estimate based on the lowest amount you have typically received in the past. It's better to budget based on the 'worst-case' scenario and add unexpected extra income into your budget later.

Tess

Tess has a gross income of £18,000. After tax and National Insurance, she takes home £1,300 per month. She gets paid on the last day of every month.

Cami

Cami works 25 hours a week at a children's shoe shop and two four-hour shifts in a bar. She is paid a total of £267 every Friday. She also collects tips on Friday and Saturday nights. Her lowest estimate is £5 per night, which comes to at least £10 per week.

Adam and Ayesha

Ayesha operates her graphic design business as a sole trader. Her profits vary each month, depending on the number of projects she finishes. She is usually able to pay herself at least £1,500 each month. She pays herself during the last week of the month. Adam earns £26,000, which means he takes home £1,775 (after deductions) on the last working day of the month. He also has a side hustle as an online English teacher. This pays between £350 and £450 a month, which arrives in his account on the first day of the month.

WHAT ARE YOUR CURRENT SPENDING HABITS?

If you are setting up a budget for the first time, you might not have a lot of data on your current spending. However, this part of the puzzle is absolutely crucial for creating a successful budget.

For example, Tess once set herself a target of spending £200 a month on food. She made an effort to select cheaper options at the supermarket but otherwise didn't really change her food-buying habits. She only got half way through the month before she had spent the £200. It wasn't until she looked back at her bank statements from several previous months that she realised her average food spend was closer to £400! She realised she would need to make big changes to the way she had been shopping to get her food spending down to where she wanted it to be. For this budget, she sets herself a goal of £350.

It is also possible to completely forget some spending categories. When creating her first budget, Cami forgot that every three months she has to buy new contact lenses. By looking at your past spending, you will be less likely to forget infrequent but necessary expenses.

Go through your bank statements for *at least* the last month and copy out every transaction. Yes, every single one. If you are trying to create your first budget for the month of June, go back at look at everything you have spent so far in May. If you can face going through the previous three to four months that's even better because your first budget will be a more accurate reflection of your true spending. You can use the spending log in the free Mindful Budget Bundle[3] download, or a blank piece of paper.

---

[3] https://downloads.grace-allison.com/mindful-budget-bundle

If you *really* don't have the time or patience to tally up all of your past spending, I don't want you to feel like the doors are closed on your budgeting journey. You *can* use guesstimates, but be aware that your first budget might not be 100% accurate and might need some tweaking later on.

Make the commitment to track your spending, starting right now. It is much less of a chore to add the items as you spend rather than having to do it all at once at the end of the month.

Once you have all of your spending written down, divide the items into categories. Add up the amounts to find your total monthly spend in each category. Here are some examples of categories to get you started:

Food	Clothes
Household	Kids
Petrol	Gifts
Fun	Memberships
Going Out	Subscriptions
Pet(s)	Bills
Health	Hobbies
Beauty	Miscellaneous

The number of categories you will have is unique to you and your spending habits. Personally, I prefer to have fewer, broader categories, but you might prefer to break your categories down to help you understand more about where your money is going.

Does a budget always have to cover a month?

A month-long budget cycle is a good place to start if you are new to budgeting. This is because many people get paid once a month, and bills usually recur on a monthly basis. It also makes it easier to look back over bank statements, as they are issued once a month. However, different budget cycles work for different people. For example, if you get paid weekly you might prefer to work with a shorter budget cycle. I will go into more detail in Step Two about how to do this. For now, we are just gathering data on your current spending habits.

WHAT FIXED EXPENSES ARE DUE AND WHEN?

Fixed expenses are things like rent and phone bills that don't change much from month to month. The fact that they are 'fixed' doesn't mean that you can't reduce or eliminate them, it's just that you know in advance how much they will be. This is in contrast to variable expenses (which we will get to later) like food, where you have much more control over the amount you spend.

Some fixed expenses, like gas and electricity, will vary through the year. Use your 'worst-case-scenario' guesstimate based on past experience, or national averages that you can look up online. Later I will show you how to account for differences in your planned and actual spending.

Write out every fixed expense and when it is due. If you've just tallied up all of your spending for the previous month, the chances are you will have a lot of this information in front of you already.

WHAT BIG EXPENSES DO YOU NEED TO SET ASIDE MONEY FOR?

A common problem with budgeting is how to handle big and irregular expenses. Not all expenses repeat on the same schedule as our salaries, and some expenses are bigger than we can afford using a single pay check. We might budget monthly but have big expenses that come round once or twice a year. Insurance premiums, pets, birthdays and car maintenance are just some of the things that can throw up costs, often unexpectedly. They can cause big problems if we're not ready for them!

If you have ever had trouble handling big, irregular expenses then you are not alone. Tess is one of five siblings and Christmas is a really big deal in her family. Last year, she got caught out with no savings before Christmas. She ended up putting almost £1,000 on her credit card, which she is still trying to pay off. This year she plans to be a bit more careful – there will be lots of homemade presents rather than shop-bought ones, and nights in with her siblings rather than nights out! For these things, Tess wants to save £500 between this January and next December.

When she and her boyfriend adopted their puppy, Otter, Cami had no idea how expensive dogs could be. While she was still at university, Otter cut his paw on some broken glass in the park. Not only did Cami feel really guilty, but she and Mark had to pay more than £500 in vet's bills. Cami's dad eventually helped them out, but the money came at the cost of a lecture about being 'too young and irresponsible to own a pet'! Cami is determined not to let that kind of thing happen again. She wants to set a small amount of money aside on a regular basis for anything unexpected that might happen to Otter.

Every month, Adam and Ayesha have been putting as much money into their savings as they can. However, when it was time to pay for their car insurance, vehicle tax and a minor repair before their MOT, they didn't have enough money in their current accounts to pay for it. They were forced to dip into their savings. Even though they had the money that they needed, it was discouraging to deplete their savings. They agreed that they would have preferred to have put slightly less into their savings and to have an amount set aside specifically for their car.

Sinking Funds

When you set money aside for a specific purpose like a car, Christmas or a pet, it is called a sinking fund. This is different to a savings fund. A savings fund is for an event or goal in the future like a wedding, buying a house, or a one-off holiday. You put money into a savings fund and, once the time comes, you spend it.

It is unlikely, for example, that you'd start saving up for another wedding the morning after you get married! However, that is exactly how a sinking fund works. To create a Christmas sinking fund, you will add a little money to the fund every time you get paid. You will spend your Christmas money in the weeks leading up to the 25th of December. On the 26th, you'll start saving again for next Christmas.

With a sinking fund for a car or a pet, you might find yourself dipping into it at any time of the year. That's what it's there for, and that's why it's so important to keep the fund topped up. There will be more information on how to operate your sinking funds in Step Three.

WHAT DO YOU OWE IN DEBT?

I'm not going to lie – this part might be painful.

I need you to write down everything you owe. Note the minimum payments (which should also be included in your fixed expenses) and the interest rates. Add up everything.

It might be uncomfortable to see all of this written down in one place, but remember that mindful budgeting is about being honest and non-judgmental. It doesn't matter how you got into debt, the way out is to face up to your current situation and make a plan to move forward.

Tess is the only one of our budgeters who is paying off debt. She still has £931 on her credit card from last Christmas.

Student Loans

Depending on which country you are from, you may or may not want to include any student loans that you have. In the UK, you only pay back student loans once you reach a certain income threshold. Some people choose to see the repayments on these loans (currently charged at 9% of income above £26,575) as an additional tax for graduates and don't worry about making extra payments. For others, it is important to pay off the loan early to reduce the interest paid over the course of their career.

If you are from a country like the USA, where interest rates on some student loans are significantly higher, I imagine you will want to pay these debts off as soon as possible. The Mindful Budget method will show you how to do this.

Do mortgages count as debt?

In a word, yes. That doesn't make them bad; when we budget mindfully, nothing is inherently bad. There is no good debt and no bad debt, there is just debt.

Debt sometimes allows us to do things that are important to us, such as getting an education or getting on the property ladder. Hopefully both of these actions will increase our future wealth and happiness. However, debt costs money. The longer the life of your debt, the more it will cost you.

So, should you focus on making extra payments on your mortgage or putting money into savings? Take a look at the interest rates for both your mortgage and your savings. Will you get more value out of reducing your mortgage debt and the interest payments that go along with it? Or will you get more out of putting the same amount of money into a savings account and watching the interest grow?

WHAT ARE YOUR SAVINGS GOALS?

This final question brings us back full circle to the first question of the Know Your Money worksheet: Why are you making a budget?

You know what your 'why' does for you.

For Tess, her dream of cycling half-way round the world makes her so excited that just *thinking* about it keeps her up at night, the way that Christmas used to when she was a little kid. Cami is never happier than watching Otter hop from rock to rock as she and Mark walk to the base of their next climbing adventure in the Peak District. Adam and Ayesha get choked up when they talk about their plans to start a family and the home they hope to create.

That's what your 'why' does for you. Now, what do *you* need to do to make it happen? Making your dreams a reality will require your time, your energy, your creativity and, in all likelihood, some of your hard-earned cash. So let's get specific.

What?

What *exactly* will make this goal achievable? What specific financial resources will you need? Do the research. Be as accurate as you can.

How?

How are you going to make the 'what' happen? If you have decided that you will need £1,000, how are you going to save that amount? Be really specific about the changes you will make to your life and your spending habits.

When?

When do you want to achieve this goal, or when do you plan on reviewing your progress to see if you are on track?

Where?

Where are you going to keep your savings? How will you organise different savings funds held in the same account? (More on this in Step Three!)

Who?

Who can you call on for support in your financial journey? Are you working towards shared goals with a partner? Do you feel it would be beneficial to speak to a financial advisor? Do you have a close friend you are willing to share the specifics with so that you can bounce around ideas?

COMPLETED 'KNOW YOUR MONEY' WORKSHEETS FOR OUR CAST:

Tess

Here is Tess's completed 'Know Your Money' worksheet.

The Mindful Budget
Know Your Money
Work Sheet

Why? are you making a budget?

I want to quit my job and cycle from Bangkok to London with Clara!

Where? is your money?

Account	Notes	Balance
Lloyds Current	Main account, salary	£241
Lloyds Savings	Emergency Fund	£750
Credit Card	Credit Card	-£931
HSBC Current	Currently Empty	£0
HSBC Joint	Joint with Housemates	£210
HSBC Savings	Cycle tour savings	£85
	Total:	£355

How much? do you earn and when?

Source	Pay Day	Amount
Salary from the Dental Practice	Last day of the month	£1,300
	Total:	£1,300

How much? do you spend? Average for November & December

Food	Transport	Going Out
£406	£48	£53

Beauty	Clothes	Stationary
£16	£28	£21

Rent	House Bills	Credit Card
£350	£105	£27

Phone and Netflix	Gym / Yoga	
£34	£80	

What? are your fixed expenses?

Expense	Date	Amount
Rent	1st	£350
Yoga	3rd	£35
CrossFit	8th	£45
Credit Card	11th	£27
Phone Bill	15th	£28
Netflix	22nd	£6
Housemates	28th	£105
	Total:	£596

When? are your big expenses due?

January

February

March

April

May

June

July

August

September

October

November

December

Christmas!
£500

Other

How much? do you owe in debt?

Debt	Amount	Interest Rate	Minimum Payment
Credit Card	£931	18%	£27 |//
Total:	£931		£27

Savings Goals

Why?
The Cycle Tour!!

What?
Bike = £2,500
Plane Ticket = £1,200
Trip Costs = £6,000

How?
- Focus on paying off credit card.
- Only buy things on my wish list
- Less nights out, less on food
- Get back into babysitting

When?
Best time to start the trip is Jan / Feb = 12 months time. Will reassess in 3 months.

Where?
Cycle tour savings will go in HSBC savings account. Christmas Sinking Fund in HSBC current account.

Who?
Partner in crime, Clara!

Cami

Cami has to be my favourite out of all of our case studies. In the year that we follow her budgeting journey, Cami earns minimum wage and starts with less than £1,000 to her name. Considering all of this, you might be surprised at what she manages to achieve!

How much? do you spend? Based on August spending

Food	Otter	Climbing Kit
£250	£35	£75

Fun	Climbing Gym	Rent and Bills
£55	£38	£365

What? are your fixed expenses?

Expense	Date	Amount
Rent	1st	£275
Gas & Electric	1st	£21
Council Tax	1st	£62
TV license	1st	£7
Climbing Gym	1st	£38
Mobile Phone	10th	£15
Broadband	17th	£15
	Total:	£433

When? are your big expenses due?

January	February	March
		Contact Lenses £45

April	May	June
		Contact Lenses £45

July	August	September
		Contact Lenses £45

October	November	December
		Contact Lenses £45

Other

Rent = £275 per month = £69 per week
Bills for the flat = £90 per month = £23 per week
£40 per month for unexpected costs for Otter

How much? do you owe in debt?

Debt	Amount	Interest Rate	Minimum Payment

Total:

— Savings Goals —

Why?
Climbing adventures with Mark and Otter!

What?
Emergency Fund = £500
I have £100 so far
Camper Van = £1650

How?
- Small savings each week will add up
- Spend all my free time climbing so I won't be tempted to spend money!

When?
Realistic to save this amount in a year

Where?
Emergency fund and sinking funds in Barclays Savings. Camper van savings in Nationwide joint savings acct.

Who?
Mark (& Otter)

Adam and Ayesha

The couple have filled in their Know Your Money worksheet together. They will separate their joint and personal expenses when it is time to create their first budget in Step Two.

The Mindful Budget — Know Your Money Work Sheet

Why? are you making a budget?

Buy our first home in cash and start a family!

Where? is your money?

Account	Notes	Balance
Adam Lloyds	Salary and direct debits	£27
Ayesha Lloyds	Salary and direct debits	£106
Joint Lloyds	Direct debits and bills	£454
Joint Lloyds Savings	House Fund and Emergency Fund	£19,768
Adam Lifetime ISA	House Fund	£8,481
Ayesha Lifetime ISA	House Fund	£5,992
Ayesha Monzo	Variable Expenses	£5
Adam Monzo	Variable Expenses	£3
Joint Monzo	Joint Variable Expenses	£11
Ayesha Pension	Stakeholder Pension	£5,491
Joint Credit Card	Occasional use for credit score	£0

Total: £40,338

How much? do you earn and when?

Source	Pay Day	Amount
Adam Salary	Last working day	£1,300
Ayesha Salary	Last week of month	
Adam Side Hustle	1st	

Total: £1,300

How much? do you spend? Average for last six months

Food	Car	Household Supplies
£450	£220	£10

Joint Entertainment	Joint Treats	Rent and Bills
£17	£51	£727

Adam Personal	Ayesha Personal	
£295	£277	

What? are your fixed expenses?

Expense	Date	Amount
Rent	1st	£495
Utilities	1st	£60
Council Tax	1st	£130
Netflix	6th	£9
Amazon Prime	10th	£8
TV Licence	15th	£13
Internet	18th	£30
Adam Gym	1st	£28
Adam Phone	20th	£25
Ayesha Phone	20th	£18
Ayesha Pottery Studio	20th	£13
	Total:	£829

When? are your big expenses due?

January	February	March
Holiday to Spain £800		

April	May	June
Car Insurance, Tax & MOT £750		

July	August	September

October	November	December

Other

Car Maintenance = £500 over the year

Ayesha physiotherapy = £240 per year

Adam needs new clothes for new school year = £200

Adam's blog running costs = £300 per year

How much? do you owe in debt?

Debt	Amount	Interest Rate	Minimum Payment

Total:

— Savings Goals —

Why?
Building our life together with no debts!

What?
Emergency Fund = £5,000 ✓
House Fund = £115,000
Moving Fund = £5,000
Baby Fund = £3,500

How?
- £333 into both LISAs each month.
- House fund is the priority.
- Budget for Ayesha's lowest income
- Any extra into house fund

When?
Want to buy a house and start a family in next five years.
Check progress every 6 months

Where?
House fund kept in LISAs and Lloyds savings.
Sinking funds in Monzo pots

Who?
US... ♡♡♡

JOINT FINANCES

A common question for couples is whether or not they should do their budgeting together. This depends on to the extent to which they wish to combine their finances. Every couple's situation is unique.

It is helpful to think of it as a spectrum. At one end of the spectrum, you have couples who keep their money completely separate. They don't have a joint bank account. They may take it in turns to pay for items they share, or they may have a system of paying each other back. At the other end of the spectrum are couples who have no distinction between 'mine' and 'yours'. They combine all of their financial resources. All expenses are considered 'joint', regardless of who benefits from them. In between these two extremes are couples who combine some expenses but not others. They may have one or more joint accounts, which they both pay into, but they also keep a portion of their income for themselves.

Both of the couples in our examples fall into this 'in-between' category. Cami and her boyfriend keep a lot of their finances separate but they share the expenses related to their dog. They also have a joint savings account for their camper van. Adam and Ayesha are working towards shared goals, such as buying a house and starting a family. Over the years, more and more of their expenses have become 'joint' expenses, but they still keep a small amount of their own money separate. They have found this to be the best way to avoid arguments about the things that they value differently. For instance, Adam spends more money meeting his friends for drinks and meals out, while Ayesha prefers to use her money for trips to visit her friends and family who live further away.

Which way is better?

When it comes to handling money as a couple, there is no best way to do things. No one else can tell you when it is the right time to move in together, get married or to go your separate ways. In the same way, no one else can tell you to what extent you should combine your finances. The perfect balance of 'joint' versus 'separate' in your relationship will depend on the extent to which you value the same things and have the same shared financial goals.

It is certainly simpler to do everything as if you and your partner were one financial entity but it's possible to manage personal *and* joint budgets using the methods described in this book. In the next chapter, Adam and Ayesha will be creating their budget using a spread specifically designed for couples using the Mindful Budget method.

Top tip: talk about money so that you don't argue about money

It is quite common for people to avoid talking about money and it is very common for money to be a source of stress and worry. These two factors create the perfect storm for money to become the focus of resentment and arguments in a relationship.

This is because not only is it easy for the topic of money to become emotionally charged, but people haven't put in the time to learn how to talk about money with their partner. When the subject of money comes up in an argument it can get really messy, really quickly. The key is to have regular, rational, mundane, *normal* conversations about money. Money is less likely to come up in an argument because resentment doesn't get the chance to build.

It is also quite common for one person in the relationship to take on more of the budgeting burden. This is often simply because one person feels more inclined to budget. If you're the one who picked up this book, perhaps it is you! You are the one with the bullet journal, the one who organises the kitchen cabinets and remembers all the birthdays.

But I could be wrong. Maybe you are the other half of the relationship – the carefree, whimsical one who wears odd socks and writes shopping lists on their hand in biro.

These kinds of personality differences can be just as much a source of conflict when it comes to money as the money itself. Luckily a budget doesn't *need* to be beautifully laid out and embellished with washi tape. (Of course, if that's what you're into then I say, 'Go for it!') Essentially, a budget just needs to work for both people in a relationship. That involves good communication, compromise and remembering all the reasons why you love the other person.

Step Two
PLAN YOUR MONEY

This section will walk you through the process of deciding where your money will go. You will be using your information from Step One to answer the following questions:

- What budget cycle works best for you?
- What is your starting balance?
- What is your income for this cycle?
- What fixed expenses are due in this cycle?
- What will you realistically spend on variable expenses?
- What do you need to put aside for big expenses?
- What is left to put towards debt?
- What is left to put towards savings?
- What's left at the end? (Hint, it should be zero!)

Zero-Based Budget

The Mindful Budget method uses what is called a 'zero-based budget'. This means that the final balance of your budget will be zero. This doesn't mean that you will have spent every penny that you have earned, or that your bank balance will be zero, but that every penny was given a job. By the time you close your budget, all your money has gone off to do its job and there is nothing left over.

To demonstrate the Mindful Budget method, I will be going through Tess's first budget step by step. She will create her budget using the Budget Overview spreads included in the free <u>Mindful Budget Bundle</u>[4] download. For now, you can follow with your own budget using any scrap piece of paper.

Here is what the blank spread looks like:

---

[4] https://downloads.grace-allison.com/mindful-budget-bundle

Budget Overview

Cycle Dates   Starting Balance

Income

Source   Expected   Reality

Total:
Plus Starting Balance:

Fixed Expenses

Expense   Date   Expected   Reality

Total:
What's Left:

Variable Expenses

Category	Budget	Reality

Total:
What's Left:

Big Expenses

Sinking Fund	Budget	Reality

Total:
What's Left:

Debt Payments

Debt	Goal	Reality

Total:
What's Left:

Savings

Fund	Goal	Reality

Total:
What's Left:

Starting Balance + Income − Fixed Expenses − Variable Expenses

Sinking Funds − Debt Payments − Savings − Buffer = 0

Notes

Try creating your first budget using pencil rather than pen, or as a rough draft. You might find that there is a lot of crossing out and reworking as you try to get everything how you want it to be.

WHAT BUDGET CYCLE WORKS BEST FOR YOU?

Before you can get started creating your first budget, it's important that you choose a budget cycle that suits your finances. For many people the most logical option will be a month-long cycle that starts on the first of the month and ends on the last day of the month. This is the financial schedule that most of the world has adopted; your bank statements are issued monthly, many people are paid once a month and most bills are due once a month.

However, a month-long budget cycle doesn't work for everyone. Perhaps, like Cami, you are paid weekly. If you force yourself to stick rigidly to a monthly budget cycle, things can get a bit confusing. If you're unsure what cycle length is right for you, try a few different options until you find one that makes sense for your life and your finances.

WHAT IS YOUR STARTING BALANCE?

With a zero-based budget, it is important to know the starting balance of your account. Remember, *all* of your money is going to be given a job to do, including the amount that is already in your bank account.

Tess uses a monthly budget cycle and her starting balance is £241. Here is how she starts her budget off:

Budget Overview

Cycle Dates
January 2020

Starting Balance
£241

WHAT IS YOUR INCOME FOR THIS CYCLE?

Enter your expected income for this budget cycle. If you aren't sure exactly what you will be paid, use your 'worst-case scenario' estimate based on past earnings.

The Mindful Budget method adds your starting balance to your income to figure out the total amount of money that you have to work with during your budget cycle. Later you might also include money taken from your sinking or savings funds to cover big expenses. More on that in another chapter – let's not get ahead of ourselves! For now, include your starting balance and your expected income and add them all up at the bottom of the table.

Here is Tess's expected income. Underneath the total, she adds her starting balance so she knows how much money she has to budget this month.

Income

Source	Expected	Reality
Salary	£1,300	

Total: £1,300
Plus Starting Balance: £1,541

WHAT FIXED EXPENSES ARE DUE IN THIS CYCLE?

Remember, your fixed expenses are the bills, subscriptions and other payments that occur regularly. These expenses are 'fixed' in the sense that they are roughly the same every time, or because you don't really have a choice about paying them. Enter the name of the expense, the date that it is due and the amount that you expect to pay.

Fixed Expenses

Expense	Date	Expected	Reality
Rent	1st	£350	
Yoga	3rd	£35	
CrossFit	8th	£45	
Credit Card	11th	£27	
Phone Bill	15th	£28	
Netflix	22nd	£6	
Housemates	28th	£105	

Total: £596

What's Left:

The £105 that Tess must pay to 'Housemates' is the total of all the shared household bills and expenses for the month. For simplicity, she makes one single transfer at the end of the month (shown here in January), so that her share of these expenses is covered for the following month (February).

Round It Up!

You might notice that all of the examples I give in this book are round numbers, for example £3, not £2.95. I use this 'save the change' method for a few reasons. Firstly, it keeps things simple. Whether or not you are doing your finances by hand or on a spreadsheet, it is much less time-consuming to deal in whole numbers. Secondly, it is an easy, painless way of making a guaranteed savings every cycle. You won't notice 5p here and 75p there, but when you close your cycle, you will find a little stash of cash that you can put towards debt or a savings goal.

Total up everything in your fixed expenses column and subtract this total from your income. This goes in the 'What's Left?' box at the bottom of the fixed expenses. The equation is:

Total Income + Starting Balance − Fixed Expenses = What's Left?

For Tess, the equation is:

£1,300 + £241 − £596 = £945

```
Netflix         22nd         £6
Housemates      28th         £105



                        Total:    £596
                   What's Left:   £945
```

Now she knows how much money she has to carry forward into the next step; variable expenses.

WHAT WILL YOU REALISTICALLY SPEND ON VARIABLE EXPENSES?

The key word here is *realistically*. You should pick an amount for each spending category that is an accurate reflection of what you have spent in the past. Over time you can make changes to your spending habits to reduce your costs, but I would caution against setting overly ambitious goals for reductions in your spending without being clear on how you'll achieve them.

Based on her past spending, Tess sets herself the following goals for her variable expense categories.

Variable Expenses

Category	Budget	Reality
Food	£350	
Transport	£50	
Going Out	£25	
Beauty	£15	
Clothes	£20	
Stationary / Books	£20	

Total: £435
What's Left: £510

Again, total up all of your predicted variable expenses and subtract this total from what was left of your income after your fixed expenses. This goes in the 'What's Left?' box at the bottom of the variable expenses table. Now the equation looks like this:

Total Income + Starting Balance − Fixed Expenses − Variable Expenses = What's Left?

Tess's equation looks like this:

£1,300 + £241 − £596 − £435 = £510

WHAT DO YOU NEED TO SET ASIDE FOR BIG EXPENSES?

What big expenses did you list in Step One? These big expenses will make up your sinking funds. This is the part where you work out how much you need to set aside during each budget cycle for each sinking fund in order to meet these costs when they come up.

Let's use Tess's Christmas sinking fund as an example. This, her first budget, is for the month of January. She has eleven months to save up for Christmas (December doesn't count, as most of the spending will take place before she receives her December salary). She wants to have £500 for gifts, food, travel and going out money over the Christmas period. This means that she will need to save £46 each month between now and next Christmas.

Big Expenses

Sinking Fund	Budget	Reality
CHRISTMAS! – £500 in 11 months – £46 per month – Current Balance = £0	£46	
Total:	£46	
What's Left:	£464	

Just like before, total up everything that you plan to add to your sinking fund(s) and subtract this from what was left of your income after your fixed expenses and variable expenses. This goes in the 'What's Left?' box at the bottom of your Big Expenses table. Now the equation looks like this:

Total Income + Starting Balance – Fixed Expenses – Variable Expenses – Big Expenses = What's Left?

Tess's equation is now:

$$£1,300 + £241 - £596 - £435 - £46 = £464$$

Tess has £464 left to budget. This can go towards tackling her debt or saving up for her cycle tour.

WHAT IS LEFT TO PUT TOWARDS DEBT?

If you are in the process of paying off debt, you will have included all of your minimum payments in your list of fixed expenses. Once you pay off your debts, you'll no longer need to make that minimum payment. The sooner you can do this, the less interest you will pay over time. This means more money to put towards your savings goals. These are all good reasons for prioritising debt reduction over savings. So if you can, make extra debt payments whenever possible.

Tess decides to go 'all in' with this approach. She won't put any more money towards her travels until she has paid off her credit card in full.

Debt Payments

Debt	Goal	Reality
Credit Card	£364	

Total: £364
What's Left: £100

Once again, in the 'What's Left' Box underneath the Debt Payments table, we take the equation one step further:

Total Income + Starting Balance − Fixed Expenses − Variable Expenses − Big Expenses − Debt Payments = What's Left?

Tess does the maths:

£1,300 + £241 − £596 − £435 − £46 − £364 = £100

WHAT IS LEFT TO PUT TOWARDS SAVINGS?

If savings are so important, why have we left them until the end? The mistake that people make is starting with their savings goals when they try to create a budget. It's all very well to say, 'I want to save £300 every month for my savings goal.' Before you know where the rest of your money is going, however, you can't say whether or not this goal is achievable.

People typically overestimate what they can save in the short term. They set an overly ambitious goal for what they think they can put aside each month. But they still have to pay for necessities like their rent, council tax and car insurance. What ends up happening is that their variable expenses (food, fun, etc) get squeezed in the middle between their fixed expenses and their overly-ambitious goal. This either leads to them feeling deprived or to failure, neither of which is a recipe for success in the long term.

When Tess first started saving for her cycle tour across Asia, she made the same mistake. Five months before her birthday, she decided that she was going to buy her touring bike before she turned twenty-five. The bike cost £1,500 so she needed to save £350 a month – but at that point her spending habits were leaving her with only about £250 at the end of each month! Needless to say, she didn't make her goal. Then Christmas happened and she blew all her savings *and* took on credit card debt. Bummer.

That's why the Mindful Budget approach starts with life's necessities (fixed expenses, variable expenses and big expenses). After that, you work towards paying off any debt that is weighing you down. *Only then* will it become clear what you are able to save in the current budget cycle.

People might overestimate what they can save in the short term but, with truly mindful budgeting, you might *underestimate* what you can save over the next several *years* once you have a really robust plan in place.

For now, Tess isn't putting anything into savings, but she has filled in the boxes just to remind herself of her goals.

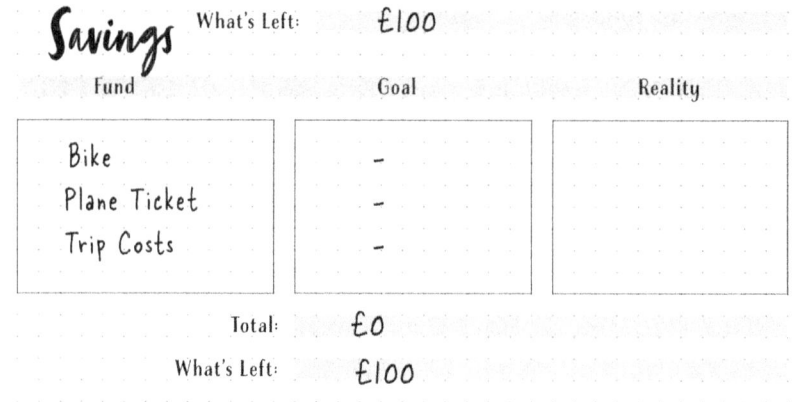

Now, to work out 'What's Left?' after savings, our equation will be:

Total Income + Starting Balance – Fixed Expenses – Variable Expenses – Big Expenses – Debt Payments – Savings = What's Left?

Tess's answer doesn't change because her savings for this month were zero:

$$£1,300 + £241 - £596 - £435 - £46 - £364 - £0 = £100$$

Buffers

It's often a good idea to have a 'buffer' amount of between £20 and £100 in each of your current accounts. A buffer is an amount of money that sits in your account so that you're less likely to go overdrawn accidentally, and so that you never have to see a scary zero on your bank balance. Tess decides that she wants to have a buffer in her account of £100, which is why it's okay that her budget still has £100 after subtracting debt payments and savings.

WHAT IS LEFT AT THE END? (HINT, IT SHOULD BE ZERO!)

Here is what we have so far:

1. Begin the budget cycle with your **starting balance**.
2. Add your **income** for that cycle.
3. Subtract your **fixed expenses.**
4. Subtract all of your **variable expenses**.

5. Subtract the amounts that you will add to your sinking funds for your **big expenses**.
6. Subtract any extra **debt payments** that you are able to make.
7. Subtract the amount, no matter how small, that you will put towards your **savings** goals.
8. Subtract your **buffer**, the balance that you will deliberately leave in your bank account.
9. The number left at the bottom of your page should be **zero**.

To double-check her working, Tess uses the boxes at the bottom of the page.

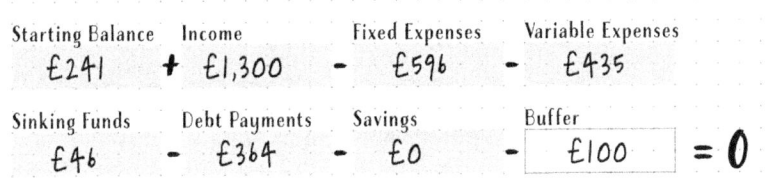

It's a good idea to do this step in pencil as your numbers may well be different by the end of the month when you will fill in the 'reality' columns.

Here is Tess's budget overview in full:

Budget Overview

Cycle Dates
January 2020

Starting Balance
£241

Income

Source	Expected	Reality
Salary	£1,300	

Total: £1,300
Plus Starting Balance: £1,541

Fixed Expenses

Expense	Date	Expected	Reality
Rent	1st	£350	
Yoga	3rd	£35	
CrossFit	8th	£45	
Credit Card	11th	£27	
Phone Bill	15th	£28	
Netflix	22nd	£6	
Housemates	28th	£105	

Total: £596
What's Left: £945

Variable Expenses

Category	Budget	Reality
Food	£350	
Transport	£50	
Going Out	£25	
Beauty	£15	
Clothes	£20	
Stationary / Books	£20	

Total: £435

What's Left: £510

Big Expenses

Sinking Fund	Budget	Reality
CHRISTMAS! -£500 in 11 months -£46 per month -Current Balance = £0	£46	

Total: £46

What's Left: £464

Debt Payments

Debt	Goal	Reality
Credit Card	£364	

Total: £364
What's Left: £100

Savings

Fund	Goal	Reality
Bike	—	
Plane Ticket	—	
Trip Costs	—	

Total: £0
What's Left: £100

Starting Balance   Income   Fixed Expenses   Variable Expenses
£241   + £1,300   − £596   − £435

Sinking Funds   Debt Payments   Savings   Buffer
£46   − £364   − £0   − £100   = 0

Notes

CAMI'S WEEKLY BUDGETS

Cami gets paid once a week so it makes sense for her to use a weekly budget cycle starting on a Monday and ending on a Sunday. Her first budget is for the week of the 31st of August to the 6th of September. On the 30th of August – a Sunday – Cami sits down to create her budget for the following week. Her income for that week is the wages that she received on Friday the 28th and any tips that she collected on Friday and Saturday nights.

Here is a copy of Cami's budget calendar. These blank calendar spreads can be found in the free Mindful Budget Bundle[5] download.

September

Monday	Tuesday	Wednesday	Thursday	Friday	Saturday	Sunday
31.	1. - G & E - Gym - C.Tax - Rent - TV license	2.	3.	4. Paid today	5.	6.
7.	8.	9.	10. - Mobile Phone	11. Paid today	12.	13.
14. Buy contact lenses	15.	16.	17. - Broadband	18. Paid today	19.	20.
21.	22.	23.	24.	25. Paid today	26.	27.
28.	29.	30.	1. - G & E - Gym - C.Tax - Rent - TV license	2. Paid today	3.	4.

Each time Cami is paid on a Friday, she assigns that income a colour. She shades each week a different colour to correspond to the income that she will use to cover her expenses that week. For example, her wages on Friday the 28th of August were assigned the colour orange. The first week of September is shaded orange, meaning that any expenses from that week are to be covered by her August 28th wages.

---

[5] https://downloads.grace-allison.com/mindful-budget-bundle

Her wages on September 4th are assigned the colour blue, so the week of the 7th to the 13th of September is shaded blue. Which wages will cover her mobile phone bill on the 10th? The 'blue' wages from the 4th of September. Easy!

To create her budget for the first week of September, Cami will use the same Budget Overview spread that Tess used for her monthly budget. The process for Cami is very similar, with a few exceptions:

1. Because she is using a weekly cycle, Cami only includes her weekly earnings in the income table.
2. Similarly, Cami only includes the bills that are due this week in the fixed expenses table. Other bills due later in the month will appear in later budgets.
3. The third major difference is Cami's use of sinking funds to cover monthly expenses that can't be covered by a single week's income.

For example, Cami's weekly income of around £277 barely covers her rent for the month, which is £275, due on the 1st. If she paid her rent all at once from her wages, she would have nothing left for her share of the household bills that are also due on the 1st, not to mention food or other necessities. Cami can avoid this problem by creating a sinking fund for her rent and her household bills. Each week, Cami puts aside £69 for rent and £23 for bills. She has a number of other sinking funds: one for her dog; one for new climbing equipment and clothes, and one for costs relating to her contact lenses.

Whenever Cami needs to take money out of her sinking funds to cover big expenses, she includes these amounts in her income table. This method allows Cami to see how much money she has to work with in her budget for the week. Notice in the first week of September how she has included amounts from her 'Rent' sinking fund and her 'Bills' sinking fund in the income table.

Budget Overview

Cycle Dates
31st August - 6th September

Starting Balance
£47

Income

Source	Expected	Reality
Shoe Shop	£202	
Bar	£65	
Tips	£16	
Rent Sinking Fund	£275	
Bills Sinking Fund	£90	

Total: £648

Plus Starting Balance: £695

Fixed Expenses

Expense	Date	Expected	Reality
Rent	1st	£275	
Gas & Electric	1st	£21	
Council Tax	1st	£62	
TV license	1st	£7	
Climbing Gym	1st	£38	

Total: £403

What's Left: £292

THE MINDFUL BUDGET

Variable Expenses

Category	Budget	Reality
Food	£65	
Otter	£10	
Fun	£15	

Total: £90

What's Left: £202

Big Expenses

Sinking Fund	Budget	Reality
Rent	£69	
Bills	£23	
Otter	£10	
Climbing Kit	£10	
Health and Eyes	£7	

Total: £119

What's Left: £83

Cami's Variable Expenses

Cami has decided on three categories for her variable spending.

Food — For Cami this includes anything bought at the supermarket as well as the occasional trip to a cafe or a pub.

Otter — This category covers Cami's share of the dog food and other consumables like vitamins, treats and poo bags!

Fun — Fun expenses for Cami include the petrol money, for when Mark drives the two of them to a climbing venue, and other luxuries like magazines and streaming movies online.

Don't let someone else's categories influence yours because this is a recipe for confusion. Use the categories that make the most sense to you.

Cami's Sinking Funds

Putting money aside for big expenses is especially important when you are paid weekly to make sure that you don't struggle when monthly bills or other irregular expenses come up. Even though Cami took money out of her sinking funds to pay for her rent and bills, she topped up these sinking funds that week, too. This way, she will be ready for the start of the next month when many of her big expenses come due again.

Cami's Savings

Cami is lucky not to have any debt, so she skips this section of the Budget Overview and carries all of 'What's Left' to savings. Cami has two savings goals: she wants to build up an emergency fund of £500, and she wants to save £1,650 to buy a camper van with her boyfriend. The emergency fund takes priority so she will put all available savings towards this fund until she reaches her goal.

Here is the page showing her expected savings for the week.

In the first week of the month, Cami expects to be able to save £33. Considering that her savings goals come to over £2000, £33 might not seem like a lot but remember that these are just her savings for a single week out of the month. Cami has fewer bills due in the second, third and fourth weeks of the month; in addition, she is usually able to make small savings in each of her variable spending categories.

By the end of September, Cami is able to save £249. That's not including the spare change that she saves by using the rounding-up method (more on this in Step Four), which she uses for treats and luxuries. You can see all of her budget spreads for each week of the month in Appendix 1.

Cami's budget is a great example of how small amounts of savings can add up quickly. We will revisit Cami's savings again in Step Four, where you can find out how much she is able to save over a longer time period.

Debt Payments

Debt	Goal	Reality

Total:
What's Left:

Savings

Fund	Goal	Reality
Emergency Fund	£33	
Camper Van	—	

Total: £33
What's Left: £50

Starting Balance Income
£47   + £648

Fixed Expenses   Variable Expenses
− £400   −   £85

Sinking Funds   Debt Payments   Savings   Buffer
£119   −   £0   −   £41   −   £50   = 0

Notes

ADAM AND AYESHA

Next up are Adam and Ayesha, who use a monthly budget cycle. Most of Adam and Ayesha's monthly outgoings are joint expenses such as rent, utilities and food. They do, however, keep some expenses separate.

Rather than having to do three separate Budget Overview spreads (one for joint expenses, one for Ayesha and one for Adam), the couple use a special Couple's Budget spread, also part of the free Mindful Budget Bundle[6] download. The great thing about this method is that it allows couples to create their joint and personal budgets alongside each other. It is easy to visualise what is going on financially across the relationship because all of the information is in one place.

The process for filling in the Couple's Budget spread is exactly the same as the Budget Overview that Tess and Cami used:

1. Begin the budget cycle with your **starting balance**.
2. Add your **income** for that cycle.
3. Subtract your **fixed expenses.**
4. Subtract all of your **variable expenses**.
5. Subtract the amounts that you will add to your sinking funds for your **big expenses**.
6. Subtract any extra **debt payments** that you are able to make.
7. Subtract the amount, no matter how small, that you will put towards your **savings** goals.
8. Subtract your **buffer**, the balance that you will deliberately leave in your bank account.
9. The number left at the bottom of your page should be **zero**.

The only difference is that you have three different budgets to account for: Budget A, Budget B and Budget C. In Adam and Ayesha's example, Budget A is for the couple's joint expenses, Budget B is for Adam's personal expenses and Budget C is for Ayesha. Let's take a look at the first page.

---

[6] https://downloads.grace-allison.com/mindful-budget-bundle

Budget Overview

Starting Balance A: £454
Starting Balance B: £27
Starting Balance C: £106

May 2020 — Dates

Income
Expected vs Reality

Source	Full Amount	Budget A	Budget B	Budget C
Adam	£1,775	£1,775		
Adam TEFL	£350		£350	
Ayesha	£1,500	£1,200		£300
Total:	£3,625	£2,975	£350	£300
	Plus Starting Balance:	£3,429	£377	£406

Fixed Expenses

Expense	Date	Expected	Reality	Expense	Date	Expected	Reality	Expense	Date	Expected	Reality
Rent	1st	£495		Gym	1st	£28		Phone	20th	£18	
Utilities	1st	£60		Phone	20th	£25		Pottery Studio	20th	£13	
Council Tax	1st	£130									
Netflix	6th	£9									
Amazon Prime	10th	£8									
TV Licence	15th	£13									
Internet	18th	£30									
	Total:	£745			Total:	£53			Total:	£31	
	What's Left:	£2,684			What's Left:	£324			What's Left:	£375	

Every time they're paid, Adam and Ayesha put most of their income in the joint account and keep a small portion for their own personal expenses. The shaded areas of the income table are for the couple's expected income:

Adam's main salary from his teaching job: £1,775
Adam's expected earnings from his side hustle teaching English online: £350
Ayesha's expected salary from her graphic design business: £1,500

These full amounts go in the 'Full Amount' column of the income table. The columns for Budgets A, B and C show how the couple plan to divide their income between shared and personal expenses.

Adam contributes all of his main salary to Budget A, the joint budget. His earnings from his second job all go to Budget B for his personal expenses. Ayesha only has one source of income; she contributes £1,200 of this to the joint budget and keeps £300 for herself in Budget C.

After income, the next section of the spread is fixed expenses. You can see how the couple have divided their fixed expenses into joint expenses, Adam's expenses and Ayesha's expenses. The totals are subtracted from the income and starting balance for each budget and 'What's Left' is carried over onto the next page.

The next two pages show Adam and Ayesha's variable spending categories, their sinking funds and their savings. The couple aren't currently paying off any debt, so this section has been left blank.

Variable Expenses

Category	Budget	Reality
Food	£400	
Fuel	£120	
Household	£25	
Treats	£50	
Total:	£595	
What's Left:	£2,089	

Category	Budget	Reality
Going Out	£75	
Looks	£25	
Learning	£50	
Blow Money	£20	
Total:	£170	
What's Left:	£154	

Category	Budget	Reality
Trips & Visits	£75	
Health	£50	
Art Supplies	£50	
Books	£15	
Total:	£190	
What's Left:	£185	

Big Expenses

Sinking Fund	Budget	Reality
Car	£101	
Audible	£12	
Holiday	£89	
Total:	£202	
What's Left:	£1,887	

Sinking Fund	Budget	Reality
Romance	£10	
Blog	£26	
Rugby	£15	
School Clothes	£17	
Total:	£68	
What's Left:	£86	

Sinking Fund	Budget	Reality
Apps	£11	
Clothes	£15	
Physiotherapy	£25	
Total:	£51	
What's Left:	£134	

The final page of the budget is a summary of all of the couple's spending areas. Like the income table, the shaded area of the box is for anticipated spending and the clear area will be filled in at the end of the month with the actual amounts. We will look at expected versus actual spending in Step Three.

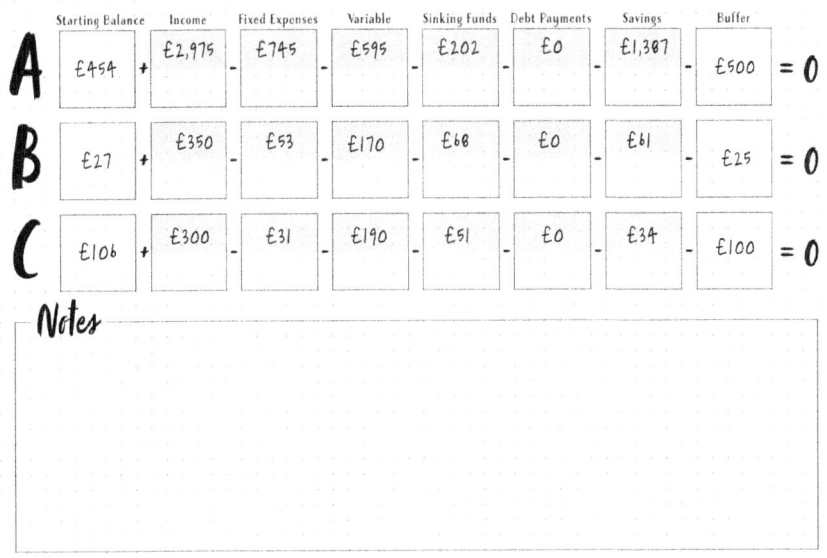

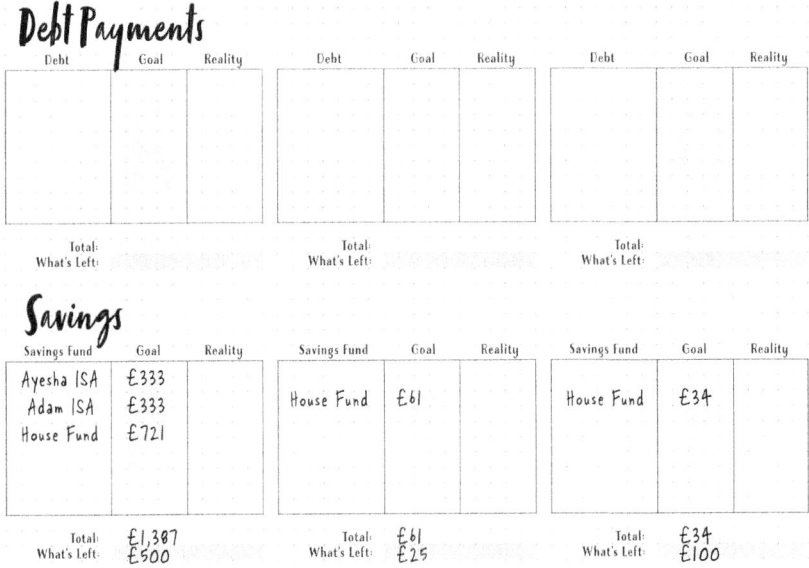

Across all three of their budgets, Adam and Ayesha expect to save £1,483 this month. Not bad! We'll catch up with them later in Step Four to find out when they can expect to achieve their savings goals.

Step Three

SPEND YOUR MONEY
(IN LINE WITH YOUR BUDGET)

It is all very well to create a budget. Once you have all of your financial information in one place (Step One: Know Your Money), I hope you'll agree that it was quite straightforward to input the numbers and then add and subtract them as necessary (Step Two: Plan Your Money). However, being able to stick to your budget in another skill entirely. Step Three of the Mindful Budget approach is about making sure that you spend your money *in line with your budget*.

This section of the book will teach you three things:

1. How to stick to your budget.
2. How to know if you are sticking to your budget.
3. How to get back on track if things aren't going exactly to plan.

To accomplish these things, we will look at three different budgeting tools that are essential to managing a successful budget.

Those tools are:
Tool #1: Spending Logs
Tool #2: Cash and Cashless Envelopes

Tool #3: Sinking and Savings Funds

At the end of the chapter, we will check in with our cast of budgeters. We will see how they managed with their first budgets and compare their expected and actual spending.

TOOL #1: SPENDING LOGS

They aren't glamorous, they aren't high-tech, but they work. Spending logs are perhaps the single most important budgeting tool that exists. If you were only going to change one thing after reading this book, I hope that it would be this: every single time that you spend money – no matter what it is, no matter how small it is – write it down. I'll say it one more time for effect.

WRITE. IT. DOWN.

Why does this make such a big difference? It is amazing how easy it is to misunderstand our spending habits when we don't keep track of them. You might have realised this for yourself in Step One when you went back over your past spending to try and gauge what you spend on different categories. Without understanding how we spend our money in the present, we cannot make a realistic plan for our money for the future.

The central idea of the Mindful Budget approach is awareness. We need to understand where our money is going. You may have dozens of transactions over the course of your budget cycle. You cannot possibly retain all of that information without recording it in some way.

But spending logs don't just increase our awareness of *where* our money is going. They are a fantastic tool for helping us gain awareness of *why* we make certain spending decisions. Let's use Tess as an example…

When we first met Tess at the start of her budgeting journey, she takes the bus to and from work every day. The way the bus timetable lines up with her work schedule on Tuesdays and Thursdays means that she often has a fifteen to twenty minute wait at the bus stop after work. During this time she will often pop into Costa for a coffee before the bus arrives. These small expenses add up over the month. It wasn't until she started tracking her spending that she noticed how much she was spending on 'after-work snacks'. Noticing the pattern helped her realise why this was happening. Now she has the option to change the habit if she wants to. Before she brought awareness to this issue she didn't even have the option to change because she didn't fully realise what was going on.

Here is an example for how to lay out your spending log:

Spending Log

Date	Day	Item	Category	Cost

One column that I often see missed out from spending trackers is 'day', as in 'day of the week'. Knowing what kind of spending takes place on a Monday versus a Saturday, for example, is really useful information. It is an excellent way to spot patterns in your spending. Patterns often indicate habits, and habits are what we will be looking to change in Step Four.

At the start of this chapter I promised that I would teach you three things:

1. How to stick to your budget.
2. How to know if you are sticking to your budget.
3. How to get back on track if things aren't going exactly to plan.

So, how do spending logs help you do these three things?

1. Sticking to your budget.

Spending logs help you stick to your budget because the simple act of recording your spending with pen and paper keeps you mindful of how you are spending your money. In addition, they help you create budgets each month that are an accurate reflection of your current spending habits. Having a realistic budget is the first step to sticking to your budget!

2. Knowing if you are sticking to your budget.

If you don't record your spending, how will you know if you have actually stuck to your budget? By updating your spending logs every day, or at least once a week, you can tell if you are staying on track with the goals you have set for yourself.

3. Getting back on track if things aren't going exactly to plan.

If you can see from your spending log that you are in danger of overspending, then you have a chance to do something about it!

Is this forever?

You might be wondering if you will need to track all of your spending for the rest of your life. That's ultimately up to you. There have been periods in my life when I have not logged my spending, or even created a budget every month. And that's okay. These were periods where I was confident (because of my past budgets) that I was living well within my means. However, whenever circumstances changed (a new job, a big life change or a new savings goal) I have fallen back on budgeting to keep me on track financially.

You are reading this because you want to learn to manage your money in a more mindful, successful way. Do the hard work of tracking your expenses now, and the skill of mindful budgeting will always be there for you to fall back on when you need it.

TOOL # 2: CASH ENVELOPES

A cash envelope is exactly what it sounds like: a real-life envelope filled with real-life cash. After spending logs, the envelope system is my favourite budgeting tool. It has been around for years but has seen a recent resurgence among Millennials. Many people who are now in their twenties and thirties have used debit cards for their entire spending lives. These same people are now starting to realise that it is all too easy to mindlessly swipe a card and let their spending get away from them.

The psychology behind this mindless spending with plastic is simple. When we use a debit card, we don't see our money leaving our account. All we see is the item we have bought. We get the impression that we have done nothing but gained from the transaction, regardless of how much (or how little!) value the item has added to our lives. However, when we spend in cash we see not just the item that we have gained but also the money that we have lost in exchange. It becomes a much more tangible process. Spending in cash primes us to think more carefully about the value of what we are buying: will you actually be better off as a result of this transaction?

You can set up a cash envelope system using any type of 'envelope' to hold your money. Don't think that you need to make a big investment in special equipment or stationery before you have had a chance to try the system. You can make the envelopes yourself out of paper and tape, or use ziplock bags. The only requirement is that the envelope is secure enough that your cash won't fall out. This is especially important if you keep coins in your cash envelopes, which you will need to if you are from a country which uses high-value coins like the £1 and £2 that we have here in the UK.

In addition to the envelope, you will need a method for writing down what you have spent from each category and how much is left. You can write these calculations on the paper envelope itself, or you can use the miniature paper spending logs from the free <u>Mindful Budget Bundle</u>[7] download. That way, you will never be left guessing how much you have left to spend in the current budget cycle.

---

[7] https://downloads.grace-allison.com/mindful-budget-bundle

Cash Envelopes in Action

Take a look at your completed budget overview. Which items *could* be paid for in cash? Chances are that most of your fixed expenses will be regular bills that need to be paid online or by direct debit. But what about your variable expenses? How many of your categories involve shopping in person as opposed to shopping online? These are the categories that make ideal candidates for the cash envelope system. If there is a spending category where you regularly struggle to stay under budget, it might be worth the effort – for a while at least – using a cash envelope for it.

Cashless Envelopes

Not everyone will feel comfortable carrying around a large amount of cash so here are a few ways around this. You can keep most of your cash envelopes at home and only bring the cash with you that you think you will need for the day. You can also make use of cash*less* envelopes.

Cashless envelopes are a way of allocating the money held in your bank account so that it can be earmarked for different purposes. One way to keep track of the envelopes is by using a paper or digital spreadsheet. You can also choose a bank that provides an envelope-type feature through their online banking. This feature goes under different names with different providers – envelopes might be called 'pots' or 'vaults', for example. High-street banks are gradually catching on to the demand for services like this, but the current leaders in the market are the newer app-based banks such as Monzo and Starling. My advice is to do some research using YouTube. Reviewers often share their screens as they demonstrate the app's functions, giving you a good idea of whether or not you like the interface.

If you choose to use cashless envelopes for some or all of your spending categories, I would still highly recommend using the miniature paper spending logs while you are out and about. This brings some of the benefits of physical cash envelopes to the cashless envelope system. The act of writing everything down by hand brings back that all-important awareness to your spending.

So, to recap, how do cash envelopes help?

1. Sticking to your budget

Cash envelopes help you stick to your budget because cash spending is more tangible than electronic spending.

2. Knowing if you are sticking to your budget

You can easily see if you are sticking to your budget because you can see how much money is left in each envelope.

3. Getting back on track if things aren't going exactly to plan

If you run out of cash in a category then you have two options. You can try and hold out until the end of the budget cycle without spending any more in that category, or you can add cash from another category or from a sinking or savings fund. With the first option, you get a little taste of deprivation to help encourage you to spend more mindfully next cycle (or to set a more realistic spending goal for that category). With the second option, the act of physically moving money from one envelope to another acts as a wake-up call that things didn't go quite right, and encourages you to do better next time. But please don't see events like this as a failure. Mindful budgeting isn't about beating yourself up, it's about constantly refining your budgeting skills to set you up for financial success in the long run.

TOOL # 3: SINKING AND SAVINGS FUNDS

The theory behind sinking and savings funds is relatively straightforward. Sinking funds involve setting aside money for big, recurring or ongoing expenses. Savings funds are for one-off needs and longer-term goals. How you manage your sinking and savings funds *in practice* is where it starts to get interesting.

Separate Bank Accounts

One way to manage different funds is to have separate bank accounts for every sinking and savings fund. However, it might not always be practical to have lots of different accounts, especially if some of your funds are for relatively small amounts. If nothing else, it's a lot of bank details to keep track of! Consider having separate accounts for a few of your bigger funds and then use some of the strategies listed below to manage your smaller funds.

Cash Envelopes

For relatively small funds, a 'cash envelope' system can work really well. For example, Cami keeps her contact lenses sinking fund in cash, in a tin on her shelf at home. Every three months, when her contact lens supply runs out, she takes the money from the tin to buy a new set.

Managing different funds within the same bank account

If you decide keep multiple funds in one bank account, then you will need a way to keep track of how the money is allocated. Here is a spread, filled in by Adam and Ayesha, to show how they keep track of their 'house' fund and their 'emergency' fund.

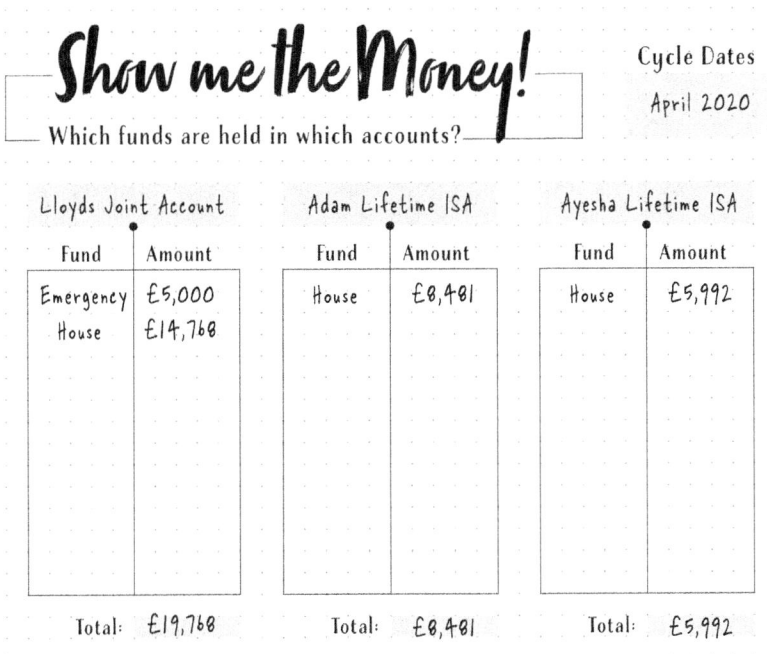

THE MINDFUL BUDGET

Sinking Fund Trackers

It is normal and expected for the balance of your various sinking funds to fluctuate. That's the whole idea; you take from it as you need, secure in the knowledge that you are using that money exactly as you intended. This means that you will need a solid method of keeping track of what goes in, out and how much you have left in each of your sinking funds.

Remember, every time you use money from a sinking fund, you add the amount to your income for that budget cycle. If you know at the start of the budget cycle that you will be using money from a sinking fund, add the amount to the 'expected' column of your income. If you need to dip into a sinking fund midway through the budget cycle, add the amount to the 'reality' column of your income.

Below, you'll find two of Cami's income tables for September. In the first one, she knows she will use her 'rent' sinking fund so it is included in her expected income. In the second, she uses her 'Otter' sinking fund for an unexpected vet bill. She adds the amount to her 'reality' income column when she closes out her budget at the end of the cycle.

Budget Overview

Cycle Dates
31st August - 6th September

Starting Balance
£47

Income

Source	Expected	Reality
Shoe Shop	£202	£202
Bar	£65	£65
Tips	£16	£16
Rent Sinking Fund	£275	£275
Bills Sinking Fund	£90	£90

Total: £648 / £648
Plus Starting Balance: £695 / £695

Budget Overview

Cycle Dates
21st - 27th September

Starting Balance
£50

Income

Source	Expected	Reality
Shoe Shop	£202	£202
Bar	£65	£65
Tips	£16	£16
Otter Sinking Fund		£48

Total: £283 / £331
Plus Starting Balance: £333 / £381

Cami also uses the following spread to keep track of her sinking funds. At the beginning and end of each budget cycle, she updates how much she has added to each fund, how much she has spent from it and the new balance.

THE MINDFUL BUDGET

Sinking Fund Progress Tracker

Fund: Date:	Rent	Bills	Otter	Climbing	
31/08	£276 £69 £276	£92 £23 £92	£35 £10	£0 £10	Start In
6/09	£69	£23	£45	£10	End
7/09	£69 £69	£23 £23	£45 £10	£10 £10	Start In
13/09	£138	£46	£55	£20	End
14/09	£138 £69	£46 £23	£55 £10	£20 £10	Start In
20/09	£207	£69	£65	£30	End
21/09	£207 £69	£69 £23	£65 £10 £48	£30 £10	Start In
27/09	£276	£92	£27	£40	End
28/09	£276 £69 £276	£92 £23 £92	£27 £10	£40 £10	Start In
4/10	£69	£23	£37	£50	End
5/10	£69 £69	£23 £23	£37 £10	£50 £10 £56	Start In
11/10	£138	£46	£47	£4	End

Savings Fund Trackers

To keep track of savings funds, I recommend two types of trackers. The first is almost identical to the sinking funds tracker shown above. It shows you how much you have put into the fund each month, any amount that you might have taken out, and the current balance.

The second type of savings tracker is a bit more fun. It allows you to shade or colour an object or text, as a visual representation of your progress. Included in the free Mindful Budget Bundle[8] download are three different savings tracker designs, as well as a blank template that you can use to create your own.

---

[8] https://downloads.grace-allison.com/mindful-budget-bundle

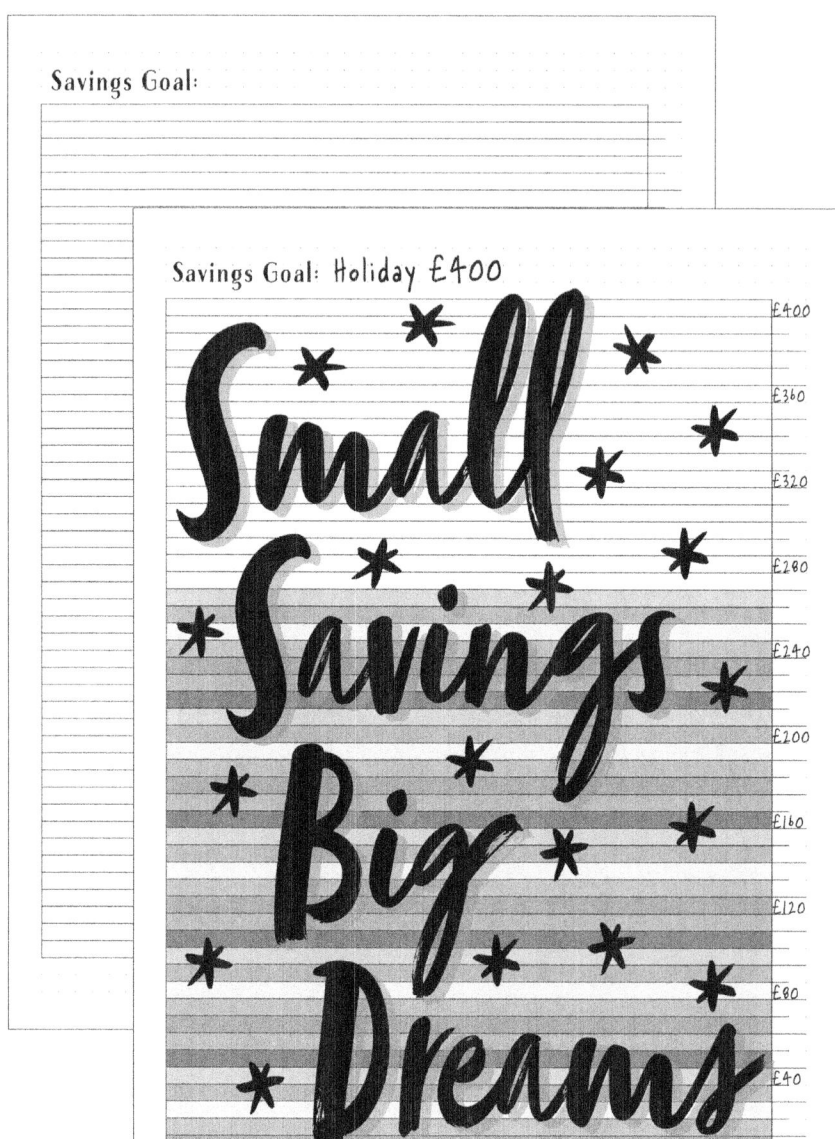

To recap; do sinking and savings funds do everything they promised?

1. Sticking to your budget

A well-managed system of sinking and savings funds helps you stick to your budget by ensuring that you have the money set aside for big expenses and future goals without relying on credit cards or loans.

2. Knowing if you are sticking to your budget

It is important to have a robust system for tracking how much is in your various funds. If you know this, then you will know if you will have enough set aside in these funds for the important upcoming events in your life.

3. Getting back on track if things aren't going exactly to plan.

Using some of your savings to build up an emergency fund is the ultimate way to get back on track. When things in life *really* don't go to plan, then you have your emergency fund to fall back on without going into debt.

How long does all of this take?

Between creating your budget, stuffing your cash envelopes, recording your spending, and managing your sinking and savings funds, you might be wondering if adopting a more mindful approach to budgeting will leave you with time for anything else!

The truth is that, yes, setting up your budgeting system can be a little time consuming at first. However, once you have found a system that works for you it takes only a small amount of maintenance to keep it going. You can choose to make it part of your daily routine, or to do a small amount of work on your budget once a week or once a month.

Closing out your budget at the end of a budget cycle and creating a new budget for the following cycle is probably the biggest time commitment. However, in my experience, once you have started to find success in managing your money, the process of budgeting becomes more and more enjoyable. And the best way to find success is to dedicate some time at the start to learning this new skill. You've got this!

BUDGET VERSUS REALITY

Creating your budget at the start of the budget cycle is an excellent way to set your financial intentions for that period. However, setting your intentions is only *half* of the process of mindful budgeting. You also need to evaluate whether or not you have done what you intended. This is where the 'reality' section of your Budget Overview spread comes in.

At the start of the budget cycle, you decided what you expected to happen with your finances for the upcoming budget cycle. You noted down your expected income, fixed expenses, variable expenses, debt payments and sinking and savings funds. At the end of the budget cycle you will update your spread to include what you actually earned, spent and saved.

Remember that the key tenet of mindful budgeting is non-judgemental awareness of your personal finances. If your budget didn't go smoothly during this cycle, learn from the experience and move forward to the next budget. There is nothing to be gained from beating yourself up about mistakes that you can't change.

In this section, we will go through the budgets of Tess, Cami, Adam and Ayesha and update them with the actual amounts earned, spent and saved.

Expected versus Reality: Income

For many people, their income varies slightly from pay cheque to pay cheque. This is the case for Ayesha's income from her graphic design business and from Adam's income from his second job as an online English teacher. In their Budget Overview, they used their 'worst-case scenario' guesstimate for their 'expected' income column (the grey shaded column). Once they know how much they have actually earned, they update their 'reality' column with their true income.

Budget Overview

May 2020 — Dates

Income

Expected **vs** Reality

Source	Full Amount	
Adam	£1,775	£1,775
Adam TEFL	£350	£395
Ayesha	£1,500	£1,950
Total:	£3,625	£4,120

Tess also has some unexpected income. In addition to her day job as a dental assistant, Tess decides to do some weekend babysitting. This helps to expedite her financial goals in two ways: she earns a little bit extra *and* she doesn't spend as much on going out because she is staying in all evening with her tiny charges! This is what her income table looks like after she updates it at the end of the month with her babysitting income.

Income

Source	Expected	Reality
Salary	£1,300	£1,300
Baby Sitting		£150
Total:	£1,300	£1,450
Plus Starting Balance:	£1,541	£1,691

THE MINDFUL BUDGET

Expected versus Reality: Fixed Expenses

The next step is to update your fixed expenses with the amounts that you actually spent. Tess's spread reflects the fact that she decided to cancel her yoga membership and reduce her mobile phone bill. In reality, her fixed expenses where almost £50 less that she expected. These drastic changes to fixed expenses might not be possible every budget cycle but are very normal at the start of your mindful budgeting journey as you decide what expenses are truly worth it.

Fixed Expenses

Expense	Date	Expected	Reality
Rent	1st	£350	£350
Yoga	3rd	£35	-
CrossFit	8th	£45	£45
Credit Card	11th	£27	£27
Phone Bill	15th	£28	£15
Netflix	22nd	£6	£6
Housemates	28th	£105	£105
	Total:	£596	£548
	What's Left:	£945	£1,143

Expected versus Reality: Variable Expenses

As the name suggests, this is the area where you are likely to see the most variability between your expected spending and your spending in reality. Here are Adam and Ayesha's variable categories for the month. Adam overspent by a few pounds in his 'learning' category, but in all their other categories the couple managed to keep their spending below their budgeted amounts.

Variable Expenses

Category	Budget	Reality	Category	Budget	Reality	Category	Budget	Reality
Food	£400	£386	Going Out	£75	£70	Trips & Visits	£75	£70
Fuel	£120	£65	Looks	£25	£21	Health	£50	£50
Household	£25	£16	Learning	£50	£53	Art Supplies	£50	£43
Treats	£50	£31	Blow Money	£20	£17	Books	£15	£15
Total:	£595	£498	Total:	£170	£161	Total:	£190	£178
What's Left:	£2,089	£2,641	What's Left:	£154	£208	What's Left:	£185	£197

Carrying over unspent cash to the next budget

If you underspend in your variable expenses categories, you have two options: you can either save the money that you didn't spend, or you can carry it over to the next month. Let's say that your food budget is £250 for the month, but that you came in under budget by £10. You can put that £10 towards a savings goal, or you can add it to your food category for next budget cycle. You would include the £10 in your income for next month and then add it to your food category in your variable spending section, bringing your food budget up to £260 for the new month.

Expected versus Reality: Debt payments, big expenses and savings

If your income, fixed expenses and variable expenses differ in reality to how you expected them to be at the time when you created your budget, then the amount you are able to put towards debt, sinking and savings funds will be different by the time you get to the end of the budget cycle.

Below you will find Tess, Adam and Ayesha's full budget overview spreads, with both their expected and actual spending for the month. All of Cami's weekly budgets for the month of September can be found in Appendix 1.

TESS'S BUDGET OVERVIEW:

Budget Overview

Cycle Dates
January 2020

Starting Balance
£241

Income

Source	Expected	Reality
Salary	£1,300	£1,300
Baby Sitting		£150
Total:	£1,300	£1,450
Plus Starting Balance:	£1,541	£1,691

Fixed Expenses

Expense	Date	Expected	Reality
Rent	1st	£350	£350
Yoga	3rd	£35	-
CrossFit	8th	£45	£45
Credit Card	11th	£27	£27
Phone Bill	15th	£28	£15
Netflix	22nd	£6	£6
Housemates	28th	£105	£105
	Total:	£596	£548
	What's Left:	£945	£1,143

Variable Expenses

Category	Budget	Reality
Food	£350	£300
Transport	£50	£25
Going Out	£25	£0
Beauty	£15	£15
Clothes	£20	£0
Stationary / Books	£20	£11
Total:	£435	£351
What's Left:	£510	£792

Big Expenses

Sinking Fund	Budget	Reality
CHRISTMAS! - £500 in 11 months - £46 per month - Current Balance = £0	£46	£46
Total:	£46	£46
What's Left:	£464	£746

Debt Payments

Debt	Goal	Reality
Credit Card	£364	£646
Total:	£364	£646
What's Left:	£100	£100

Savings

Fund	Goal	Reality
Bike	—	—
Plane Ticket	—	—
Trip Costs	—	—
Total:	£0	£0
What's Left:	£100	£100

Starting Balance Income   Fixed Expenses   Variable Expenses
£241   + £1,450   − £548   − £351

Sinking Funds   Debt Payments   Savings   Buffer
£46   − £646   − £0   − £100   = 0

Notes
- Started baby sitting again
- Cancelled yoga monthly class pass
- reduced data allowance on phone plan
- Only cooked Japanese food on the weekends
- nights in with Clara! (no going out)
- No new clothes until the summer

All money left over goes towards debt until it's gone!

ADAM AND AYESHA'S BUDGET OVERVIEW:

Budget Overview — May 2020

	Starting Balance A	Starting Balance B	Starting Balance C
	£454	£27	£106

Income (Expected vs Reality)

Source	Full Amount	Budget A (Expected)	Budget A (Reality)	Budget B (Expected)	Budget B (Reality)	Budget C (Expected)	Budget C (Reality)
Adam	£1,775	£1,775	£1,775				
Adam TEFL	£350	£395		£350	£395		
Ayesha	£1,500	£1,950	£1,200	£1,650		£300	£300
Total:	£3,625	£4,120	£2,975	£3,425	£350	£395	£300	£300
Plus Starting Balance:			£3,429	£3,879	£377	£422	£406	£406

Fixed Expenses

Expense	Date	Expected	Reality
Rent	1st	£495	£495
Utilities	1st	£60	£55
Council Tax	1st	£130	£130
Netflix	6th	£9	£9
Amazon Prime	10th	£8	£8
TV Licence	15th	£13	£13
Internet	18th	£30	£30
Total:		£745	£740
What's Left:		£2,684	£3,139

Expense	Date	Expected	Reality
Gym	1st	£28	£28
Phone	20th	£25	£25
Total:		£53	£53
What's Left:		£324	£369

Expense	Date	Expected	Reality
Phone	20th	£18	£18
Pottery Studio	20th	£13	£13
Total:		£31	£31
What's Left:		£375	£375

Variable Expenses

Category	Budget	Reality
Food	£400	£386
Fuel	£120	£65
Household	£25	£16
Treats	£50	£31
Total:	£595	£498
What's Left:	£2,089	£2,641

Category	Budget	Reality
Going Out	£75	£70
Looks	£25	£21
Learning	£50	£53
Blow Money	£20	£17
Total:	£170	£161
What's Left:	£154	£208

Category	Budget	Reality
Trips & Visits	£75	£70
Health	£50	£50
Art Supplies	£50	£43
Books	£15	£15
Total:	£190	£178
What's Left:	£185	£197

Big Expenses

Sinking Fund	Budget	Reality
Car	£101	£101
Audible	£12	£12
Holiday	£89	£89
Total:	£202	£202
What's Left:	£1,887	£2,439

Sinking Fund	Budget	Reality
Romance	£10	£10
Blog	£26	£26
Rugby	£15	£15
School Clothes	£17	£17
Total:	£68	£68
What's Left:	£86	£140

Sinking Fund	Budget	Reality
Apps	£11	£11
Clothes	£15	£15
Physiotherapy	£25	£25
Total:	£51	£51
What's Left:	£134	£146

Debt Payments

Debt	Goal	Reality

Total:
What's Left:

Debt	Goal	Reality

Total:
What's Left:

Debt	Goal	Reality

Total:
What's Left:

Savings

Savings Fund	Goal	Reality
Ayesha ISA	£333	£333
Adam ISA	£333	£333
House Fund	£721	£1,273

Total: £1,387 £1,939
What's Left: £500 £500

Savings Fund	Goal	Reality
House Fund	£61	£115

Total: £61 £115
What's Left: £25 £25

Savings Fund	Goal	Reality
House Fund	£34	£46

Total: £34 £46
What's Left: £100 £100

	Starting Balance	Income	Fixed Expenses	Variable	Sinking Funds	Debt Payments	Savings	Buffer	
A	£454	+ £2,975 / £3,425	− £745 / £740	− £595 / £498	− £202 / £202	− £0 / £0	− £1,387 / £1,939	− £500	= 0
B	£27	+ £350 / £395	− £53 / £53	− £170 / £161	− £68 / £68	− £0 / £0	− £61 / £115	− £25	= 0
C	£106	+ £300 / £300	− £31 / £31	− £190 / £178	− £51 / £51	− £0 / £0	− £34 / £46	− £100	= 0

Notes

- Aysh had a good month – £450 of extra income!
- Didn't take the car out as much on the weekends – almost halved fuel costs
- Total of £2,100 towards the house!!

Step Four

SAVE YOUR MONEY

The fourth step of the Mindful Budget approach to becoming a skilled budgeter is all about saving your money. My philosophy here is to focus on the *act* of saving, not the *amount* that you manage to save.

For example, if you have £5 left over at the end of the month it might seem pointless to put it into a savings fund. What will £5 get you, anyway? You might as well spend it now on something that your will enjoy because surely that's the only way to make the most out of such a small amount of money, right?

Wrong! Here is why it is important to save even that £5.

What you are doing when you transfer that £5 into a savings fund is *building a habit*. You might not have much to put towards savings at this point in your life but, hopefully, that won't always be the case. You are on a financial journey where you are working towards being a more mindful budgeter and spending less on unnecessary things. As you progress on this journey you will have more and more to save. You want to make sure that habit is in place well before your financial situation improves. What is more, your financial situation is *more likely* to improve if you focus on developing the discipline to save now, even when the amounts are small.

In this chapter, I will share three tips for saving more:

1. Save more by… Chasing the savings' high
2. Save more by… Changing your spending habits
3. Save more by… Using savings challenges

At the end, we will fast forward our cast of mindful budgeters to see how much they are able to save over the weeks, months and years using the Mindful Budget method.

1. SAVE MORE BY … CHASING THE SAVINGS' HIGH

If you have ever succeeded in implementing a new fitness routine, you will already understand this phenomenon first hand. It can be hard dragging yourself to the gym early in the morning, or forcing yourself to go for a run after a hard day at work. But the exercise produces feel-good chemicals in your body that make it easier and easier to work out every day. Like Pavlov's dog, drooling in the knowledge that a tasty treat is on its way, your body remembers how good it feels to work out and, over time, you experience less and less resistance.

The same is true for savings. Every time you make a cash deposit or a transfer to your savings account, no matter how small, you get a teeny, tiny hit of these feel-good chemicals. Over time, this builds a better and better relationship to saving and you will want to do more and more to feel that buzz again. It's certainly healthier and cheaper than a lot of other habits!

However, this feel-good effect only works if you let it. If you grumble and groan about 'only' being able to save £5, it will drown out any satisfaction. Give that little buzz a chance to be heard by making an effort to congratulate yourself and to feel grateful for any amount saved. It will add up in the long run. Filling in savings trackers like these are a great way to get a little dopamine hit every time you add to your savings!

Remember!

Remember that the sooner you get rid of debt, the less that debt will cost you over time, and the more you will have to save in the future.

2. SAVE MORE BY ... CHANGING YOUR SPENDING HABITS

This chapter is not about the details of what you need to do to spend less. There are countless resources online dedicated to teaching you how to save on specific categories of spending like food, pets, kids or beauty. The Mindful Budget approach believes that you already know what you need to do to spend less. *You* are the expert on your own life. You are the only one who knows whether a purchase truly brings you value.

That doesn't mean that it will be easy to make changes to your habits. Humans are fundamentally resistant to change. Sure, we love progress and improvement, but the change needed to get there can be uncomfortable. This makes sense from an evolutionary standpoint. You've always done things a certain way and, so far, you have never been eaten by a tiger. Why risk doing things differently all of a sudden?

The only way to get past this resistance is to acknowledge it. Once you have acknowledged that your mind is throwing up resistance to change, you can really begin to scrutinise it. Part of becoming a mindful budgeter is continuously reviewing the way you do things and being willing to change what isn't working. It's easy to say 'I need at £45 haircut every month because...' and give a reason. Your reason might be totally valid, but that doesn't mean that there aren't any alternatives. You will never discover those alternatives unless you are willing to entertain the idea that change is possible.

For this next step in the Mindful Budget method, you will need your spending log from your last budget cycle. This is where you recorded every single penny that left your wallet or your account. Bills, food, memberships ... everything. I need you to go through the list and, for every single item, imagine what it would look like to spend less on that thing. It doesn't mean that you have to follow through on anything at this point. Just *imagine* how things could be different.

It might help to de-personalise the process. If it is too difficult to imagine making changes, try imagining another, hypothetical person. You could give her a name – let's call her Frugal Francis. For every item on your spending log, imagine how Frugal Francis might do things differently.

Your morning coffee on the way to work costs you £3. Frugal Francis would make her own in a thermos. Yoga class during your lunch break costs you £9. Frugal Francis did a free YouTube yoga video first thing in the morning and goes for a walk in the fresh air at lunch time.

By the end of this exercise you may feel a certain degree of animosity towards Frugal Francis and her oh-so-virtuous spending habits. That's okay. At least you have come up with ideas for spending less on specific items in your personal budget.

Now I want you to revisit the very first question that you answered in Step One of this book. What is the reason that you are making a budget? Really sit and think about that thing, that dream or those people in your life that are the reason you are on this financial journey. What would you be willing to change for the sake of your 'why'?

Would you be willing to drink home-made coffee from a thermos if it brought you closer to that once-in-a-lifetime adventure? Would you be willing to do all your workouts for free from your living room if it was part of the solution to buying your home with your partner a year or two earlier?

When you frame things in terms of your 'why', change doesn't seem so bad after all. Go back to all the ideas you came up with in the first part of the exercise. Which of those habit changes would you now be willing to try?

3. SAVE MORE BY ... USING SAVINGS CHALLENGES

When you are first starting out on your savings adventure, it can be helpful to use savings challenges. It can be a fun way to motivate you to save a bit extra. You might be surprised by how much you can save by doing this kind of thing.

Save The Change

As I mentioned in Step Two, I prefer to use whole numbers in my budget (£4 instead of £3.15) for example. Not only does this make the writing and working-out quicker and easier, but it means that you are effectively setting aside the extra change for savings.

How does this work in practice?

Let's say that Cami spends £12.45 on dog food from her 'Otter' Envelope. On her spending log, she writes the amount down as £13. Cami paid for the dog food with a £10 and £5. She gets two £1 coins and 55p in small change. Cami puts the £1 back into her Otter Envelope but the 55p goes into a separate coin pouch, away from the rest of her cash envelopes. At the end of the day, Cami tips all of the small change out of the coin pouch and into a jar that she keeps on her bookshelf. She can use the money in the jar either for treats that she wouldn't otherwise have or, when the jar gets full, she can take it to the bank and deposit all of the change into her savings account, which, as you can imagine, is really satisfying!

Adam and Ayesha use Monzo, an online bank that you access through a smart phone app. Like many online banks, Monzo offer a 'rounding-up' feature. Every time the couple make a purchase with their Monzo card, the amount is automatically rounded up and the change placed in one of their 'pots'. Adam and Ayesha were able designate which pot receives the change. They have chosen for the change to go into their 'Treats' pot. They find they can enjoy those extra treats all the more because they saved the cash bit by bit, while sill sticking to their budget goals.

Tess's bank doesn't offer a rounding-up feature, but she still wants to take advantage of the 'save-the-change' method. So she does it herself! When she makes a debit card purchase, she rounds the cost up to a whole number. At the end of the month when she closes out her budget, her workings come to zero, as they should. However, the balance of her account is £105.81. Where did this 'extra' money come from? Remember, Tess has a buffer of £100 in her current account. This means that she has decided to always keep a minimum balance of £100 to avoid accidentally becoming overdrawn. The additional £5.81 is made up of the small amounts of change from each time she rounded up an expense. Tess transfers the £5.81 into her savings account. It might not sound like a lot, but Tess feels good imagining how much lamb stew that will buy in Tajikistan on her cycle tour!

The £2 Coin Rule

Every time you are given a £2 coin in change by a cashier, store it separately from your other envelopes. Put it straight in a designated £2 jar when you get home. When that's full, deposit it in your savings account. A jar full of £2 coins is not only pleasingly heavy, but it can be worth a decent amount of money. If you live in a country without a £2, use a similar denomination like a $5 bill.

No Spend Days

Once you have been tracking your spending for a while, you might notice that you are spending significantly more on certain days of the week. It might be down to going out on Friday night, getting bored and shopping online on a Sunday, or trying to beat the mid-week blues with some retail therapy on the way home from work on Wednesday.

Try challenging yourself to not spend anything at all on those days. You might find that you save money just by forcing yourself to mix up your schedule. For the best chance of success, try replacing your spending on these days with another activity that feels like a treat but doesn't cost anything. A long, luxurious bath or setting up a FaceTime call with a good friend are examples of ways to make sure that you don't feel deprived as you try and stick with this challenge.

Make-a-Wish-List

A wish list is a fantastic way to curb impulse buying. Create a challenge for yourself; if you see something you like, resist the urge to buy it until it has been on your wish list for a certain period of time. Keep track of where you saw the item and how much it costs. Most importantly, record how long you have wanted the item for. Then, when you decide it is time for a treat, you can consult your wish list. Items that have been on your list the longest have priority.

Putting time into creating a well-organised and beautiful wish list is really satisfying. This sense of satisfaction can help alleviate some of the need for instant gratification that comes from impulse buying. Make sure that you regularly update your wish list; if there is something on there that you are no longer that bothered about – get rid of it! The fewer items you have, the sooner you will get to buy the things that will truly bring value to your life.

HOW MUCH CAN THEY SAVE?

At the beginning of this book, I introduced you to four individuals and their personal financial goals: Tess, the dental nurse from Bristol, with her dreams of an epic overland adventure; Cami, the recent graduate from Sheffield, who hasn't managed to find her first engineering job yet, but is determined to make the most of her time and her money; Adam and Ayesha, a couple who have big goals of buying their first home without a mortgage and starting a family. Let's see how they get on in the long run.

Tess

In her first budget, we saw Tess make some changes to her lifestyle and expenses. She reduced her bills by signing up for a cheaper mobile phone plan and cancelling her yoga membership to do yoga at home instead. She also started babysitting at weekends and going out less. With all of these changes she was able to put over £600 in that first month towards her credit card debt.

If she carried on like this, it would take Tess less than three months to pay off her credit card bill in full. This would give her extra money to spend and save because she would no longer be required to pay the minimum amount on her credit card every month. But what about her other goals?

Tess originally wanted to save up for her cycle tour in a year's time – twelve months. If she continues to save around £600 a month, will this be possible? Unfortunately, no. It would take more like a year and a half to save nearly £10,000 that Tess needs for her new bike, plane ticket and food and accommodation costs on the road. But that's okay. Mindful budgeting involves constant re-evaluation of our goals to see whether or not we are on track. Tess doesn't see this as a failure, in fact, her revised timeline works out rather well.

The best time of year for the girls to set off on their trip (due to the weather in the different countries they will travel through) is January. Tess won't make her initial goal of being ready in January 2021, so Tess and her travel buddy Clara eventually postpone their trip until January 2022. That gives Tess twenty-four months in total to save up for the adventure. With these extra savings, Tess is able to buy a better, lighter bike, and have additional savings to act as a cushion for when she returns from her trip and is ready to look for a new job.

Cami

Cami is able to save between £200 and £250 every month. It takes her just over two months to build her £500 emergency fund. It takes her and Mark around eight months to save up for their camper van. They spend the summer kitting it out, by which time Cami has saved a further £800, and they are able to take their first trip to the South of France. They return in time for Cami to start her first full-time job at the end of August. Their next savings goal is a climbing trip to Yosemite National Park in California!

This could have been a really rough year for Cami. It has taken her fourteen months to find her first full-time job after she graduated, which, unfortunately, is not an unusual story for the graduates of today. However, when Cami looks back on this year, instead of it being the year when she received rejection after rejection for the dozens of positions she applied for every week, this was the year when she learned to manage her money, and bought an awesome camper van!

Adam and Ayesha

Adam and Ayesha certainly have the most ambitious goal of all of our mindful budgeters. Buying a house, even in the relatively affordable area in the north of England where they live, generally costs over £100,000. You might be wondering if the couple wouldn't be better off taking out a mortgage and buying sooner rather than later. They would be paying off their mortgage rather than paying rent, adding to their own equity rather than a landlord's.

Yes, from a strictly financial perspective, this might be the best option. However, mindful budgeting takes into consideration all of the factors that we use to make decisions about our money. Perhaps the couple have personal, more emotionally driven reasons for wanting to be outright home owners rather than mortgage payers. Perhaps one of them experienced losing a home as a child because of missed mortgage payments. Perhaps as a freelancer, who plans on having a baby in the near future, Ayesha is aware of how inconsistent her income can be.

Economists like to point out how irrational we are when it comes to our financial decisions but I see it differently. Emotions are important. As long as we are aware of them, and their impact on our world view, emotions deserve to be honoured in our decision making. Adam and Ayesha choose to buy a home in cash because it is the option that gives them the greatest peace of mind.

So, how long will it take? The couple have already been saving for the past three years and have put aside almost £30,000 in their Lifetime ISAs and other savings accounts. They still need around £100,000 to buy a home and cover the associated home-buying and moving fees. If the couple can continue saving around £2,000 every month, it will take them just over four years to achieve these goals.

Four years might sound like a long time. But, if you look at the couple's budget, it is hardly four years spent in misery! The couple can still enjoy life visiting family, going out with friends and pursuing their hobbies. Four years of enjoying their life as a young couple, dreaming of their future home and family? Sounds pretty good to me.

If buying a home in this way isn't for you, that's absolutely fine. The Mindful Budget method doesn't choose your goals for you, it gives you a framework for making your own goals a reality, whatever they are.

Step Five
ENJOY YOUR MONEY

Congratulations, you have done the hard work, you have put in the time. You have been over the examples and worked through the Mindful Budget method with your own information. You have created your first budget. In doing so, you have taken steps to become a more skilful, mindful budgeter.

What next? The final step of the Mindful Budget approach is all about learning to enjoy your money. Ultimately, the purpose of budgeting is to reduce the stress surrounding money. The first four steps of the Mindful Budget achieve this by helping you take back control of your spending and creating a plan for your money that supports your passions. But to truly let go of financial stress requires us to get philosophical for a moment.

Get ready, because I'm about to land you with some seemingly incompatible ideas and try and persuade you that they are all, in fact, true.

1. Money isn't real
2. Money is very real indeed!
3. Saving your money allows you to enjoy your money
4. Spending your money allows you to enjoy your money
5. Worry about the small things so that you don't have to worry about the big things

6. Don't worry about the small things
7. Sometimes you just need a cookie

Money isn't real

Money isn't real. It's an abstraction, a representation of other things in life. As a society, we decided it was a pain in the neck to cart sacks of grain through the streets every day to trade for the goods and services that we needed. Instead, we invented money to be a convenient stand in for everything else in life that has a value.

It's really important not to confuse money with the value that it represents. The money itself is not the goal. Money represents material goods that make our lives easier and more colourful, it represents time with the people we love. It represents peace of mind. A truly mindful budget doesn't lose sight of the value that lies behind the figures.

When you find yourself stressing about money, ask yourself what is the value *behind* the money that you're really stressed about. Do you not have enough leisure time? Are you afraid of uncertainty? Once you identify the true source of your anxiety, you can stop blaming nebulous 'money problems' and start working on solutions that address the root cause.

Money IS real

Despite the fact that money isn't real, money is very real indeed! By this I mean that it is a very real fact of life. Unless you live in a remote and lonely corner of the world, money is always going to be a feature of your life. A mindful budgeter doesn't have to make their life all about their personal finances but, given that money isn't going anywhere anytime soon, we might as well learn as many skills as possible to make our money work for us and our goals.

Enjoy your money by saving it

Having a clear vision of your 'why' in life allows you to set goals that truly motivate you. Saving is one of the most satisfying things that you can do with your money because it brings you closer to those goals. It also means that your money will be there for you if things don't go to plan.

Enjoy your money by spending it

To truly let go of money stress you have to be able to enjoy spending your money. Spending money is *literally* unavoidable. If you are so focused on saving, saving, saving that you experience anxiety or guilt every time you need to make a purchase, it is a recipe for a stressful and unhealthy relationship with money.

A mindful budgeter knows what things in life bring them joy. Spending wisely and intentionally on these things is not a problem. By making a robust, well-thought-out budget, you will be able to enjoy the things you buy because you know that everything else is taken care of. No more guilt, no more doubt.

Worry about the small things

One of the reasons that people put off making a budget is because they are overwhelmed. There are too many details, and the time and energy adds too much stress to their already busy lives. Remember, having a solid, mindful budgeting routine is not about *stressing* over the details, it's about *paying attention* to the details. Worry about the small stuff in your budget so that you don't *need* to worry about the big stuff. Putting a small amount of cash into a sinking fund for a pet every week might seem like too much emphasis on insignificant details. However, when a big expense like a vet bill comes up, there will be less worry in the long run.

Don't worry about the small things

As important as it is to pay attention to the details, it is just as important to know when to let go of the small things. You might misplace a £5 note, or forget to cancel a subscription that you no longer use. There is only one way deal with losses like this, big or small – if you don't have the power to change them, simply learn from your mistake and move on. It is never worth the stress of agonising over what has happened to your money in the past. Instead, channel that energy into something else that you can *actually control*, like next cycle's budget.

Sometimes you just need a cookie

A mindful approach to your budgeting does NOT mean that you have to become some kind of miserly Scrooge, who sits in the middle of an empty room wearing nothing but a hair shirt and meditating all day on how little you have spent. You are allowed to splash out and treat yourself, and cookies are the perfect metaphor for this.

Cookies are entirely pointless. They are not required for survival or enlightenment. They aren't healthy and they aren't sophisticated, they just taste really, really good. Your cookie might be a going to see a film in the cinema, even though you will be able to stream it at home in just a few months. Your cookie might be getting your legs waxed even though its winter and no one will see them, just because it makes you feel confident. Your cookie might be a taxi instead of the bus when you are tired and just want to go home.

A truly mindful budgeter knows the value of a cookie. So whatever your cookie looks like, go out and enjoy it. Enjoy your cookie, enjoy your money, enjoy your life.

Appendix 1

CAMI'S SEPTEMBER BUDGETS

Budget Overview

Cycle Dates
31st August – 6th September

Starting Balance
£47

Income

Source	Expected	Reality
Shoe Shop	£202	£202
Bar	£65	£65
Tips	£16	£16
Rent Sinking Fund	£275	£275
Bills Sinking Fund	£90	£90
Total:	£648	£648
Plus Starting Balance:	£695	£695

Fixed Expenses

Expense	Date	Expected	Reality
Rent	1st	£275	£275
Gas & Electric	1st	£21	£18
Council Tax	1st	£62	£62
TV license	1st	£7	£7
Climbing Gym	1st	£38	£38
Total:		£403	£400
What's Left:		£292	£292

Variable Expenses

Category	Budget	Reality
Food	£65	£63
Otter	£10	£9
Fun	£15	£13
Total:	£90	£85
What's Left:	£202	£207

Big Expenses

Sinking Fund	Budget	Reality
Rent	£69	£69
Bills	£23	£23
Otter	£10	£10
Climbing Kit	£10	£10
Health and Eyes	£7	£7
Total:	£119	£119
What's Left:	£83	£89

Debt Payments

Debt	Goal	Reality

Total:
What's Left:

Savings

Fund	Goal	Reality
Emergency Fund	£33	£41
Camper Van	—	—

Total: £33   £41
What's Left: £50   £50

Starting Balance   Income
£47   +   £648

Fixed Expenses   Variable Expenses
− £400   −   £85

Sinking Funds   Debt Payments   Savings   Buffer
£119   −   £0   −   £41   −   £50   = 0

Notes

- Switched Otter's food to own-brand
- Saved all £2 coins from cash envelopes = extra £4!
- Save the Change = £1.41 for little treats jar

Budget Overview

Cycle Dates: 7th–13th September

Starting Balance: £50

Income

Source	Expected	Reality
Shoe Shop	£202	£202
Bar	£65	£65
Tips	£18	£18

Total: £285 £285
Plus Starting Balance: £335 £335

Fixed Expenses

Expense	Date	Expected	Reality
Mobile Phone	10th	£15	£15

Total: £15 £15
What's Left: £320 £320

Variable Expenses

Category	Budget	Reality
Food	£65	£68
Otter	£10	£7
Fun	£15	£11

	Total:	£90	£86
	What's Left:	£230	£234

Big Expenses

Sinking Fund	Budget	Reality
Rent	£69	£69
Bills	£23	£23
Otter	£10	£10
Climbing Kit	£10	£10
Health and Eyes	£7	£7

	Total:	£119	£119
	What's Left:	£111	£115

Debt Payments

Debt	Goal	Reality

Total:
What's Left:

Savings

Fund	Goal	Reality
Emergency Fund	£61	£65
Camper Van	—	—

Total: £61   £65
What's Left: £50   £50

Starting Balance   Income   Fixed Expenses   Variable Expenses
£50   **+**   £285   **−**   £15   **−**   £86

Sinking Funds   Debt Payments   Savings   Buffer
£119   **−**   £0   **−**   £65   **−**   £50   **= 0**

Notes

- Overspent on food because of pizza night with Mark – worth it!
- Saved all £2 coins from cash envelopes = extra £2
- Save the Change = £2.28

Budget Overview

Cycle Dates
14th-20th September

Starting Balance
£50

Income

Source	Expected	Reality
Shoe Shop	£202	£202
Bar	£65	£65
Tips	£11	£11
Health & Eyes Sinking Fund	£45	£45

Total: £323 — £323
Plus Starting Balance: £373 — £373

Fixed Expenses

Expense	Date	Expected	Reality
Broadband	17th	£15	£15
Contact Lenses		£45	£45

Total: £60 — £60
What's Left: £313 — £313

Variable Expenses

Category	Budget	Reality
Food	£65	£61
Otter	£10	£8
Fun	£15	£14
Total:	**£90**	**£83**
What's Left:	£223	£230

Big Expenses

Sinking Fund	Budget	Reality
Rent	£69	£69
Bills	£23	£23
Otter	£10	£10
Climbing Kit	£10	£10
Health and Eyes	£7	£7
Total:	**£119**	**£119**
What's Left:	£104	£111

Debt Payments

Debt	Goal	Reality

Total:
What's Left:

Savings

Fund	Goal	Reality
Emergency Fund	£54	£61
Camper Van	—	—

Total: £54 £61
What's Left: £50 £50

Starting Balance Income   Fixed Expenses Variable Expenses
£50   + £323   − £60   − £83

Sinking Funds   Debt Payments Savings   Buffer
£119   − £0   − £61   − £50   = 0

Notes

- Spent less on food by making big batch of veggie curry!
- No £2 coins this week :(
- Save the Change = £1.36 in treat jar

Budget Overview

Cycle Dates: 21st - 27th September

Starting Balance: £50

Income

Source	Expected	Reality
Shoe Shop	£202	£202
Bar	£65	£65
Tips	£16	£16
Otter Sinking Fund		£48

Total: £283 / £331

Plus Starting Balance: £333 / £381

Fixed Expenses

Expense	Date	Expected	Reality
Unexpected Vet Bill	23rd		£48

Total: £0 / £48

What's Left: £333 / £333

Variable Expenses

Category	Budget	Reality
Food	£65	£63
Otter	£10	£9
Fun	£15	£10

	Budget	Reality
Total:	£90	£82
What's Left:	£243	£251

Big Expenses

Sinking Fund	Budget	Reality
Rent	£69	£69
Bills	£23	£23
Otter	£10	£10
Climbing Kit	£10	£10
Health and Eyes	£7	£7

	Budget	Reality
Total:	£119	£119
What's Left:	£124	£132

Debt Payments

Debt	Goal	Reality

Total:
What's Left:

Savings

Fund	Goal	Reality
Emergency Fund	£74	£82
Camper Van	–	–

Total: £74 £82
What's Left: £50 £50

Starting Balance | Income | Fixed Expenses | Variable Expenses
£50 + £331 − £48 − £82

Sinking Funds | Debt Payments | Savings | Buffer
£119 − £0 − £82 − £50 = 0

Notes

- Unexpected vet bill - used Otter Sinking Fund
- Saved £2 coins from cash envelopes = £2
- Save the Change = £2.19

Printed in Great Britain
by Amazon